PRAISE FOR *PATHS TO WHOLENESS: FIFTY-T*

"David Bookbinder is one of those awakened souls whose near-(timeless eyes. He has taken that gift and poured it into *Paths to Wholeness: Fifty-Two Flower Mandalas*, using innovative photography and heartfelt reflection to surface and praise the mysteries of the inner world."

— Mark Nepo, *The Book of Awakening* and *The Endless Practice*

"David Bookbinder's Flower Mandalas contain both the shock of recognition and the delight and surprise of originality. They are flowers and jewels at the same time. They will enrich anyone's feelings about what a flower is."

— Harold Feinstein, *One Hundred Flowers* and *The Infinite Rose*

"More than just an arresting coffee table book, *Paths to Wholeness: Fifty-Two Flower Mandalas* also serves as a guide for successfully traversing the hills and valleys of our existence. The photography is stunning and the short essays that accompany each image are drawn from David's considerable life experience, spiritual and therapeutic training, and innate and accumulated wisdom."

— Lama Marut, *A Spiritual Renegade's Guide to the Good Life* and *Be Nobody*

"A fascinating body of work. Absolutely mesmerizing."

— Brooks Jensen, *LensWork* magazine and *Looking at Images*

"*Paths to Wholeness: Fifty-Two Flower Mandalas* is itself a mandala — a symbol of wholeness. I experience David's nurturing each time I read it, feeling his presence as a fellow traveler and seasoned counselor. He encourages our growth as we move forward in our own journeys, healing our wounds and loving more deeply."

— Lori Bailey Cunningham, *The Mandala Book: Patterns of the Universe*

"David Bookbinder's *Paths to Wholeness: Fifty-Two Flower Mandalas* is an invitation to join him on a journey of exploration into the deepest levels of being."

— Barry M. Panter, MD, *Creativity & Madness Conferences*

"The words compelling, engaging, moving, and powerful only hint at the profound gifts contained in this beautifully written, authentic and unusual memoir/photography/mandala book. It is almost too rich to take it all in, in one or two sittings. Savor each essay and take time to absorb the richness of this collection."

— Joan Klagsbrun, *The Focusing Institute*

PATHS TO WHOLENESS

FIFTY-TWO FLOWER MANDALAS

BY DAVID J. BOOKBINDER

TRANSFORMATIONS PRESS

Paths to Wholeness: Fifty-Two Flower Mandalas

ISBN: 978-0-9846994-0-7

Mail: David J. Bookbinder
                Transformations Press
                85 Constitution Lane
                Danvers, MA 01923
Phone: 978-395-1292
Email: transformations@davidbookbinder.com

Websites: davidbookbinder.com/books
                flowermandalas.org

Social media: facebook.com/groups/pathstowholeness
                facebook.com/flowermandalas
                instagram.com/flowermandalas

Publisher's Cataloging-in-Publication data

Names: Bookbinder, David J., author.
Title: Paths to wholeness , fifty-two flower mandalas / by David J. Bookbinder
Description: Includes bibliographical references. | Danvers, MA: Transformations Press, 2016.
Identifiers: ISBN 978-0-9846994-0-7 (pbk.) | 978-0-9846994-1-4 (ebook) | LCCN 2016916833
Subjects: LCSH Mandala. | Mandala--Pictorial works. | Meditation. | Spiritual life. | BISAC BODY, MIND &
SPIRIT / Mindfulness & Meditation | BODY, MIND & SPIRIT / Inspiration & Personal Growth.
Classification: LCC BL604.M36 .B66 2016 | DDC 203/.7--dc23

"Forgiveness Meditation" written by Jack Kornfield. Used by permission.
Chöd practice adapted from *Feeding Your Demons: Ancient Wisdom for Resolving Inner Conflict*, by Tsultrim Allione.
"Personal Craziness Index" adapted from *A Gentle Path Through the Twelve Steps*, by Patrick J. Carnes.

Printed in the United States of America.

For my teachers:
Linda Kuehl, who got me writing,
Herb Mason, who taught me writing from the heart,
Gene Garber, who showed me teaching with poise,
James Grant, who helped me see,
Harold Feinstein, who opened my eyes to flowers,
and
Thich Nhat Hanh, who helped me be.

If we could see the miracle of a single flower clearly, our whole life would change.

  - Jack Kornfield

What does seeing clearly mean? It doesn't mean that you look at something and analyze it, noting all its composite parts; no. When you see clearly, when you look at a flower and really see it, the flower sees you. It's not that the flower has eyes, of course. It's that the flower is no longer just a flower, and you are no longer just you.

  - Maurine Stuart

A flower blossoms for its own joy.

  - Oscar Wilde

ACKNOWLEDGMENTS

Paths to Wholeness: Fifty-Two Flower Mandalas would not have happened without assistance from many people. I am grateful to them all.

A Massachusetts Cultural Council grant in Photography encouraged me to take myself more seriously as an artist and helped to fund the creation of many of these images.

The helpful folks at the UBC Botanical Gardens site identified some of the flowers the images are based on.

My mailing list subscribers, Facebook fans, and blog subscribers provided an encouraging and receptive audience for the Flower Mandala images and for early drafts of the essays that accompany them.

Several friends consistently read and commented on the essays, notably Barbara Drake, Larry 'Doc' Pruyne, Pat Sylvia, Barrie Levine, Elizabeth Enfield, and especially Davida Rosenblum, who not only read my first drafts but also edited the second drafts.

Finally, special thanks are due to these generous supporters whose faith in this book led them to back The Flower Mandalas Project on Kickstarter.com:

Angels:
Barbara Drake, Kathleen Murphy

Special Supporters:
Paul Bookbinder, Pearl Bookbinder, Trish Randall

Supporters:
James Harrington, Monica Andrews, Sarah Bookbinder

Contributors:
Beth A. Fischer, Beverly Butterfield, Charles N. Gordon, Deborah D'Amico, Deborah S. Strycula, Florence Sterman Schott, Grady McGonagill, Jennifer Badot, John D. Lennhoff, Josephine Lo, Kai Vlahos, Karie Kaufman, Mark Bookbinder, Mary Gail Ranaldi, Michel Coste, Rick Alpern, Sandra K. Atkins, Shelley McGarry, Susan Hand

Thanks:
Analesa BatShema, Anita Shorthill, Beilah Ross, Briana Duffy, Jane Pasquill, Jennifer Flynn Bernard, Jim and Iris Grant, Michael O'Leary, Michele Anello, Paul Lessard, Perry McIntosh, Redmund Godfrey, Sadhbh O'Neill, Susan Lennox, William Sheehan, William Z. Zwemke

CONTENTS

FOREWORD

For as long as I can remember – and that's a long time – I've been attracted to mandalas. I've amassed a large number of books about mandalas, some by mandala artists and scholars and others about nature and sacred geometry. I've even written a couple of my own! But this book of David's is like nothing I've come across before. *Paths to Wholeness: Fifty-Two Flower Mandalas* is itself a mandala – a symbol of wholeness. It is a collection of soulful stories and lovely art that intertwine and come full circle to create a brilliant whole.

I like stories, especially those which bring me a new perspective or a deeper understanding and appreciation of life. Often, the stories that offer the most meaning are those involving a hero's journey – a quest that takes us through the familiar territories of challenge, struggle, surprise mentors, unexpected gifts, and moments of deep despair. The successful quest culminates in a hard-won transformation that benefits the quester as well as the quester's community. The sacrifices and hard work of making choices and daring to act on them result in transforming the individual into a hero. Yet hero status doesn't come easy and is not guaranteed. As David points out in Chapter 40, "Perseverance": "Getting up and doing it again – persevering – is the hallmark of the hero." In *Paths to Wholeness*, David offers an intimate look into journeys he has taken – replete with challenges, struggles, triumphs, new perspectives, and the wisdom gained. At moments in which he pauses to consider his actions and reactions to a particular event or situation, I cannot help but feel a kinship with him as I consider my own responses to various life junctures. As I read his work and study his mandalas, I am drawn to engage in a strangely interactive experience – one that reminds me that while our lives are uniquely our own, they are also inextricably linked to every other being's life in some way.

I began Chapter 36, "Path," on a typically chilly November day in the Pacific Northwest. Already moved by previous chapters, I was primed for being open to what this one had to offer. I soon realized that I was in a situation similar to that which David describes in this chapter: I was at a crossroads and somewhat frozen as to which path to take. Reading the chapter rewarded me with penetrating clarity. David was pointing toward a path guided by "heart," and that gentle nudge helped me to move forward on what had been a long period of immobility with regard to a personal "heart" project. I can honestly say I experienced an opening that day, not only in response to Chapter 36, but to the entire blend of fragrant words and images contained within this book. It is, after all, a book of mandalas, and the very nature of its design is that all parts are inseparable.

David refers to himself as a late bloomer who now helps others tend to their own gardens. I experience his nurturing each time I read *Paths to Wholeness*, feeling his presence as a fellow traveler and seasoned counselor. He encourages our growth as we move forward in our own journeys, healing our wounds and loving more deeply.

- Lori Bailey Cunningham

INTRODUCTION

Your vision will become clear only when you look into your heart. Who looks outside, dreams. Who looks inside, awakens.
- Carl Jung

Paths to Wholeness: Fifty-Two Flower Mandalas came about because my numbers were in alignment. When I began it, I'd just turned 60, was almost 20 years out from a life-altering event, and had been a psychotherapist for nearly 10 years. My intention was to distill into one volume what I'd gleaned from these experiences. As often happens with art, creating it brought about something more.

The path to the Flower Mandalas themselves goes back to 1993, when a series of medical errors nearly took my life. At the time I was an English grad student at the University at Albany. What happened in a hospital there, which included a near-death experience, divided my life into two parts: who I had been and who I was becoming. To paraphrase the Grateful Dead, it's been a long, strange trip since then.

Ten years later, in 2003, I was still sorting out who that second David was. I was living in Gloucester, MA, and walked Good Harbor beach nearly every evening, usually at around sunset. It had been almost 25 years since I'd done any serious photography, but I found myself yearning to record the patterns of color and light I saw there, so I bought my first digital camera and took it with me on my walks.

I found this round of picture-taking to be a much different experience than the one I'd had back in the '70s, when I was shooting street scenes in Manhattan and Brooklyn in harsh, grainy black-and-white. Then, I'd felt like a thief, grabbing and hoarding moments of unsuspecting people's lives. Now, I felt more like a painter, taking in and reflecting on the slowly shifting landscape of light. I started carrying a camera nearly everywhere I went.

Because the image quality of early digital cameras was not up to what I was used to seeing with 35mm film, I taught myself how to manipulate images on my computer, hoping to improve them. I soon realized that once a file was on my hard drive, I could do anything I wanted with it.

Experimentally, I used an image editing program to transform photos of the clouds I'd been shooting into mandala-like images. I enjoyed both the effect and the process, so I tried it on images of other things – rocks, wood, textures. Then, I wondered what would happen if I "mandalaized" something that was already mandala-like and used the technique on a photo of a dandelion seedhead. That impulse led to my first Flower Mandala, which accompanies the essay "Acceptance."

Each of the Flower Mandalas is derived from a flower snapshot I took as I walked through various neighborhoods, visited botanical gardens and flower shops, and spotted interesting flowers in the homes and gardens of people I knew. The process of going from flower photograph to finished mandala can take anywhere from a few hours in a single session to a sequence of multi-hour sessions spread out over two or three months. Working on the images at the pixel level feels like I'm reacquainting myself with the world I saw through magnifying glasses and microscopes as a boy, what William Blake called the "minute particulars." At its best, the experience is a meditation.

I began making these mandalas at a time of personal turbulence. My choice of the hexagram as the underlying shape was initially subconscious, but I don't believe it was accidental. Like the mandala form itself, the hexagram appears in the art of many cultures throughout world history. Composed of two overlapping triangles, it represents the reconciliation of opposites: male/female, fire/water, macrocosm/microcosm, as above / so below, God and man. Their combination symbolizes unity and harmony – qualities I needed then, and took wherever I could find them. That the hexagram is also called the Star of David was not lost on me.

Early in the process of creating the Flower Mandalas, I met with a painter who had been making mandalas for years. She suggested that each of these images was trying to tell me something. "Listen to what they're saying," she advised. So I hung prints around my apartment and made them the digital wallpaper on my computer desktop.

My painter friend was right. I discovered that looking at these images completed a loop: The mandala-making process distilled a feeling just below my awareness into something more distinctly felt, and looking at the completed mandala brought that enhanced feeling back into me, purified and amplified. With each iteration of the creating/receiving cycle, I felt a little more whole. The Flower Mandalas were more than merely another way to tinker with images. They were part of a continuing reintegration process that helped remedy the shattering aspects of my brush with death and its consequences. Listening to what they were telling me helped put the pieces of Humpty Dumpty back together again, a process essential to my later becoming a psychotherapist.

A year or two later, I began to think about a weekly meditation book that matched Flower Mandalas with a concept and a relevant, meditative quotation. I briefly looked at preexisting symbolic significances for flowers, such as the Chinese and 19th century British and American languages of flowers, but I didn't resonate with them, so I went with my own associations. The process of matching Flower Mandalas to concepts was subjective and intuitive. Sometimes a mandala led me to a matching concept, and sometimes a concept led me to a matching mandala.

The quotations came to me in a similarly subjective manner. Many of them were pivotal at some point in my life and helped to initiate a permanent change in perspective. Others I took from authors I've long admired. A few I discovered only after I started this book, the quotes coming to me from chance comments, something I happened to be reading, or Internet quotation sites.

Once I matched images and quotes, I realized that I, too, had something to say about these concepts. The essays in this book have been a way to discover what I feel and think. I began each with a brain dump quickly poured out onto a blank screen. Then, as I wrote and rewrote, the real knowing began, with each pass through the text homing in on what was there to express.

The essays have continued an integrating process that began in the first moments following my near-death experience. "Acceptance" is chapter one because acceptance initiated a transformative shift – accepting that the path I'd been on as an English graduate student and aspiring fiction writer, though I'd been on it a very long time, was no longer my path, and that I had to embrace the one I was actually on. The remaining topics are in alphabetical order, the order in which I wrote them.

The structure of this book reflects how I experience internal change. Most of my major shifts in perspective began in a single moment, but it has taken a lifetime to turn insights into lasting alterations of thought, feeling, and action. The instantaneity of clicking a shutter, represented here by the Flower Mandala images, reflects the felt experience of insight. The linear flow of reading and writing, represented here by the quotations and essays, reflects the necessity of walking through time in order to fully enact new ways of being.

Two years after my near-death experience, I was in a support group for people who had survived near-death. I was still finding my way back into this world, and although I believed I had returned from the edge with something of value, I was also profoundly disoriented. Responding to my confusion, one of the group members made a wide half-circle gesture with his arm and said, "David, I think you're one of those people who has to take the long way 'round." He paused, his arm fully outstretched. "But when you get there," he said, closing his hand into a fist and pulling it to his chest, "it'll be important."

What I do now as an artist, writer, and therapist does feel important. Through these skills, I hope to render a boon that, had I not taken that long, strange trip, I would never have been able to deliver.

Carl Jung, one of the fathers of modern psychology, believed mandalas are a pathway to the essential Self and used them with his patients and in his own personal transformation. In this book, I hope to carry on Jung's tradition of using art as a means for healing and personal growth – the primary purposes it has served for me.

- David J. Bookbinder

1. ACCEPTANCE

It's all part of it, man.
  - *Jerry Garcia*

Dandelion Head

ACCEPTANCE: IT'S ALREADY THERE

My path to acceptance has been mainly through loss: lost career opportunities, relationships, health and, nearly, the loss of my life. Acceptance has come with the recognition that each loss has also been an opening.

A major turning point occurred several years ago. At that time I was bleeding internally and before I noticed any symptoms, I had already lost about 25% of my blood supply. Though less drastic than a brush with death a few years before, this situation recalled the terror of that time. I grew steadily weaker and underwent a series of increasingly invasive tests, but no diagnosis or treatment emerged. I consulted alternative healers and frantically scanned the Internet. I imagined fatal outcomes. And then one day I stopped fretting.

A Buddhist friend had given me this prayer, with instructions to recite it often, without judgment:

Please grant me enough wisdom and courage to be free from delusion. If I am supposed to get sick, let me get sick, and I'll be happy. May this sickness purify my negative karma and the sickness of all sentient beings. If I am supposed to be healed, let all my sickness and confusion be healed, and I'll be happy. May all sentient beings be healed and filled with happiness. If I am supposed to die, let me die, and I'll be happy. May all the delusion and the causes of suffering of sentient beings die. If I am supposed to live a long life, let me live a long life, and I'll be happy. May my life be meaningful in service to sentient beings. If my life is to be cut short, let it be cut short, and I'll be happy. May I and all others be free from attachment and aversion.

At first, welcoming disease or death scared me even more, but with each recitation, I grew calmer. While I waited for test results, I began to have a different relationship with time. Whether I would live or die, whether I would heal by myself, with interventions, or not at all, was already out there in my future, waiting for me to arrive. I didn't have to plan. I didn't have to do anything differently. I just had to move through time, making the best choices I could, until my fate became clear. I stopped looking things up on the Internet and returned to my work as a therapist.

That moment of acceptance was liberating. Since then, I have been increasingly able to generalize the process. It's all, already, there. I don't need to fret. I don't need to push. I just need to live my life to the best of my ability and, of the infinite possible futures, I will inevitably arrive at the one that is mine.

If there is one main factor that divides those of us who do not change from those who do, I think it is acceptance: of who we are, how we got to where we are, and that we – and only we – have the power to free ourselves.

Acceptance is being who we are, in each succession of present moments, swayed neither by avoiding what we fear nor by clinging to what we think we can't live without. In the absence of acceptance, there can be no forward movement. The hidden patterns that create clinging attachment and fearful aversion take over, repeating themselves in our minds, feelings, behaviors, and relationships. We grow older, and the external circumstances of our lives change, but inside it's, as the Talking Heads put it, "the same as it ever was, same as it ever was, same as it ever was."

Acceptance is the door that closes one life chapter and allows another to open. Acceptance is the last of Elizabeth Kubler Ross's five stages of loss and a necessary precursor to moving on from mourning. Acceptance is the first of the 12 steps in addiction recovery programs and essential to beginning a sober life. Acceptance of self, and of responsibility for change, is the start of true recovery from the many unhappinesses that may come our way. Acceptance can be painful, but it is a pain that unburdens. In difficult circumstances, acceptance is the thing most of us try hardest to sidestep – and then try even harder to achieve. In its simplest form, acceptance is saying to ourselves, "Although I may be suffering, I can be content now. Yes, there are things I would like to change, and when I change them my life may have more ease, but I can already be content with my current circumstances."

Accepting our real state, no matter what it is, begins the shift from victim – of external circumstances, of thoughts and feelings, of physical challenges, of past injuries – to victor.

2. Action

Actions speak louder than words.

  - *Unknown*

Blue Globe Thistle

ACTION: SOMETIMES INSIGHT IS THE LAST DEFENSE

At times I feel like a Sherlock Holmes of the mind, each of my clients the faithful and resourceful Watson of his or her own unsolved mystery.

A Holmes-like insight is the province of traditional psychotherapy, and it is often a helpful tool. Insight can clarify the causes of anxiety or depression, relieve guilt and shame, explicate the roots of trauma, and point the way to new and better lives. But insight alone is seldom enough to effect lasting change. And, as one of my former professors remarked, "Sometimes insight is the last defense."

In therapy, as in life, actions are more powerful than words. Identifying dysfunctional patterns, self-sabotaging thoughts, and triggered feelings that keep us prisoners of our problems is an important, even vital, preparatory step, but for significant growth, we need, also, to change what we do.

Psychologist Jim Grant envisions our collections of patterned thoughts, feelings, and behaviors as akin to a Spell that can lead us to act in ritualized, self-defeating ways. To break the Spell, we need to alter our actions. Even a slight shift in an old pattern opens the way for future growth that no amount of additional insight, by itself, can foster.

For example, addicts typically follow a limited but compelling set of commands such as: "Once I get the idea in my head, I have to get high," or "If I'm around it, I have to do it," or "Getting high is the only thing I have to look forward to." In therapy, addicts can identify triggers, challenge addiction-related thoughts, and work through the feelings that entrap them in addictive behaviors. But to break the addiction Spell, they also have to *act* differently, "faking it till they make it" even when every conscious thought and habituated emotion is screaming at them to use. They must, to paraphrase Eleanor Roosevelt, do the thing they think they cannot do.

What holds true for addiction applies to any of the maladies that bring people to therapy. Each of us has our own patterns of thought, feeling, and behavior, and each requires not just insights – words and ideas – but also *actions* to replace dysfunctional patterns with new, more fulfilling ways to be in the world.

Of course, acting differently is much easier said than done.

When I was a junior in college, I took a class in the writings and teachings of the Armenian-Russian mystic G. I. Gurdjieff. One of Gurdjieff's chief precepts was that most of us live in a waking dream, believing we are far more in control of our fates than we really are. The other students and I rejected this notion – we were, after all, the generation that would change the world! So our instructor challenged us with what seemed, at first, like trivial attempts at behavior modification.

Our first assignment was around eating. If we normally cleaned our plates at each meal, he said, we were to leave a bite behind, and vice versa. This task seemed undemanding, but in the week between classes, none of us succeeded in accomplishing it more than once or twice. Humbled but unbroken, we theorized that eating behaviors might be too deeply ingrained for an initial experiment. So next time, he let us choose. I decided to use my left hand for something I normally did with my right – opening doors – and on the way out I confidently opened the classroom door left-handed. By our next meeting, I was not so confident. I'd remembered the assignment only for that night. Score: Habit 2, David 0.

Or so I believed at the time.

What I hadn't realized then, but understand now, is that although little had changed, I had changed *something*. I *did* remember to leave a bite on my plate at least once, and I *had* opened at least one door – the classroom door – with my non-dominant hand. I just hadn't sustained the changes. Now, after witnessing hundreds of people better their lives by learning to act differently, I know that even a single exception to a dysfunctional pattern can be more potent than dozens of repetitions. Each exception makes more exceptions possible, opening the door (with either hand) to a new direction.

I have been drawn to action-oriented schools of therapy, and I use them with my clients, but psychotherapy is not the only way to break a Spell. All we need is a method that empowers us to recognize self-defeating patterns, to identify what those patterns want us to do, and to choose, through any means available, to do otherwise. And then, above all, to repeat the change again and again, as often as we can remember, until it becomes the way we live.

3. ANGER

Treat your anger with the utmost respect and tenderness,
for it is no other than yourself.

- *Thich Nhat Hanh*

Pale Yellow Gerbera Daisy

ANGER: HEAVEN AND HELL

As I emerged from a childhood depression, my first strong emotion was anger. I remember listening to Jimi Hendrix, loud, a foot away from the speakers so that the music rocked my entire body, feeling almost grateful for the Vietnam War because it gave me something to focus my anger on. Anger was energy, and at that time it may even have been life-saving, though looking back, I see that it was also imprisoning.

That is the nature of anger. Anger is difficult.

Many of us act out anger to "make the other person feel the way I do." But even if we accomplish that goal, instead of the understanding we crave, a mutually damaging struggle usually ensues.

Reenacting anger is portrayed as an alternative. In the movie *Analyze This*, Billy Crystal plays a psychiatrist who tells Robert De Niro, his mobster patient, to "just hit the pillow" when he's angry. De Niro pulls out his pistol and fires several rounds into the pillow on Crystal's office chair. Crystal pauses, smiles uneasily, then asks, "Feel better?" De Niro shrugs. "Yeah, I do," he says. Hitting the pillow *is* preferable to hitting a person. But although letting off steam can help us feel better momentarily, it can also amplify anger and create further barriers to its resolution.

Suppression – holding anger in, "biting your tongue," "sucking it up" – also has its costs. Anger turned inward leads to depression, builds walls between people, promotes passive aggression, or explosively surfaces elsewhere.

So what *can* we do with our anger?

We can, as Buddhist teacher Thich Nhat Hanh suggests, relate to it as if it were a baby in distress, crying for help. Once I asked an eight-year-old boy who was often murderously enraged at his mother how he would treat this anger if it were a baby crying. "I'd pick it up and see if it wanted to be held." And if it kept crying? "I'd try giving it a bottle." And if that didn't work? "I'd see if it had a poopy diaper." To deal with our anger, we need to find out if it wants to be held, fed, or has a poopy diaper. Then we can give it the attention it requires. Only then can we safely bring our grievances to those with whom we are angry.

In my therapy practice, I use a technique developed by couples counselor Harville Hendrix to help people with the crying babies of their anger. At the beginning of a couples or parent/child session, I explain that here, they can each fully express their anger, but instead of going back and forth, arguing as they usually do, they'll take turns: One person will speak while the other listens actively, and then they will reverse roles.

I ask the first listener to be ready to hear what the first speaker says without reacting, withdrawing, or defending, even when something feels hurtful or sounds "wrong." Then we begin. The first speaker tells his or her story and the listener mirrors it, one chunk at a time, to make sure he or she "got" it. This process continues until all the important parts of the story have been heard, mirrored, and understood. Then, the listener summarizes it all, making a kind of intellectual sense of it: "So, now that I hear how you experienced what I did/said, I can understand why you're angry." Often, the listener also empathizes: "In your shoes, I'd be angry, too." Sometimes an apology ensues: "I'm sorry I hurt you. I didn't mean to. I don't want to cause you pain." Tears may flow. Something has shifted.

After the speaker has been heard, understood, and empathized with, listener and speaker change roles. The process ends when each party has spoken and has also been heard. At that point, reconciliation often begins. Over time, this speaking/hearing process can create a durable container to hold the sometimes violent feelings that occur between people. Similar techniques have been used successfully in areas of great historical conflict such as the Middle East, Latin America, and Ireland.

Anger can feel empowering, but only its resolution is a liberation. Author Ken Feit illustrates the difference: "Once a samurai warrior went to a monastery and asked a monk, 'Can you tell me about heaven and hell?' The monk answered, 'I cannot tell you about heaven and hell. You are much too stupid.' The warrior's face became contorted with rage. 'Besides that,' continued the monk, 'you are very ugly.' The warrior gave a scream and raised his sword to strike the monk. 'That,' said the monk unflinchingly, 'is hell.' The samurai slowly lowered his sword and bowed his head. 'And that,' said the monk, 'is heaven.'"

4. ATONEMENT

The beginning of atonement is the sense of its necessity.
  - *Lord Byron*

Iceland Poppy

ATONEMENT: RELEASE, RECONCILIATION, REDEMPTION

On the first Yom Kippur after my near-death experience, I was living in Albany, NY, in a house owned by an elderly couple who had survived the Holocaust. They'd taken me under their wing, apparently seeing in my tribulations an echo of their own. Although I was no longer a practicing Jew, on this Day of Atonement they invited me to participate in a brief ceremony. We walked to a nearby creek where we joined other members of their small congregation, most of them also Holocaust survivors. Each of us wrote what we perceived to be our sins and regrets on a piece of paper, then we tore the notes to bits and tossed them into the creek. We watched the water carry them away and returned to my landlord's house for lox and bagels.

Yom Kippur is a day of fasting and reflection, a solemn one for Jews, the most holy day of the year – the "Sabbath of Sabbaths." It was especially poignant that year, six months past the most pivotal moment of my life. This Yom Kippur was not, for me, so much about confessing the year's sins and seeking forgiveness, as is traditional, as it was about facing the larger errors I had made, and the need to change direction. It was a day to revisit everything, acknowledge where I'd gone wrong, and clear the slate to make way for a new life more akin to my nature and purpose. It was also the first step on my path to becoming a therapist.

To apologize is to express sorrow at causing suffering. Atonement carries apology to the next level. To atone is also to express remorse and repentance and to make amends for that suffering, if possible.

Atonement happens not only on Yom Kippur but everywhere and everywhen. It is a powerful healing force. An example: A mother yells at her child as she herself was scolded, then catches herself, holds that child in her arms, wipes away the child's tears, and vows to act differently the next time she is angered. In these actions, she heals not only the child's hurt, but also, perhaps, the child within her, as the compassion that flows from her atonement falls also on her own inner

child. Another: The 4th through 12th steps in addiction recovery programs embody atonement and repentance. Those who embark on that path take inventory of their character, scrutinize their experience, acknowledge their wrongdoings and shortcomings, make amends whenever possible, and carry forward to others the spiritual gains they have achieved.

Just as the bumper sticker says it is never too late to have a happy childhood, so it is never too late to atone.

When I was nearly 41 and my mother 70, she came to Albany to help me in the early stages of recovery from the near-fatal events I'd recently endured. Defying my father's wishes for her to stay in Buffalo with him, instead she spent two weeks taking care of me, and in that time showed her loving attention and told me how sorry she was for the mistakes she had made in raising me. Her atonement reopened our hearts and helped to reverse decades of mutual hostility. In the many years since then, we have argued exactly twice, and only briefly. Recently, she asked me to write her eulogy. Now, I can.

Like my mother's, my own atonement has also taken time. With help from Facebook, I've reconnected with my high school girlfriend and with the woman I lived with during my Albany experience, both of whom I had planned to marry and both of whom I left. With trepidation, I wrote them to express my sorrow for things I'd done when we were together, and for how things between us had ended. My intent was not to ask forgiveness (though that is what I received), but to try to heal any lingering wounds. The effect was to bridge the gap of many years and make way for new friendships to emerge.

In my work as a therapist, I make use of the lessons I have learned from atonement. My errors and my efforts to atone for them help me guide clients to forgiveness and self-forgiveness, and to moving on from regret, guilt, and shame. Paying the lessons of atonement forward brings forth a sense of redemption.

5. AWARENESS

Nobody sees a flower – really – it is so small it takes
time – we haven't time – and to see takes time, like to
have a friend takes time.

   - Georgia O'Keeffe

Yellow Sunflower

Awareness: Birthright

In August, 2003, I attended a five-day, mostly silent retreat with Buddhist teacher Thich Nhat Hanh (and 900 others). I thought of it as "Buddhist boot camp." We awoke at 5:30 a.m., exercised with Thich Nhat Hanh or one of his monks or nuns, and spent the day meditating, listening to dharma talks, participating in discussions of Buddhist thought, and in general immersing ourselves in Buddhist practice.

At that time the older brother I never had, my close friend Robert, was in a bad way. Like me, he had nearly died about ten years before, and like me had struggled with his infirmities. For a long time, he did well, but in recent months he'd fallen into a deep depression. I was also battling depression at that time and it strained my limited emotional resources to be with Robert. In the best of times, our relationship was 70% Robert, 30% David. Lately, it had been 99% Robert, and I'd been avoiding him. But as I drove past his apartment in Gloucester on the way back from the retreat, I realized I felt healed. I could see Robert again.

When I arrived home, there was a message on my answering machine from Robert's ex-wife. I called her. "I hope you're not going to tell me what I think you're going to tell me," I said. "I am," she said. "Robert committed suicide two weeks ago."

The next day, I came down with a high fever and a severe cough. For 10 days, I was in a delirium of what turned out to be pneumonia. When I'd recovered enough to venture outside, I took a walk on Good Harbor beach. As I crested the first dune, I was overcome by the sensation that I, as well as the air, the surf, the sand, the sky, and the people and dogs playing on the beach, were all just matter and energy. Everything was a continuum, the boundary between myself and the sand and the air vague and indistinct, as if we were all images in a Pointillist painting. For the first time in my life, I not only knew but *felt* and *saw* that I was part of everything and so was everything else. I was more aware than I have ever been.

After I got home, I remembered how Thich Nhat Hanh had described the beauty of the retreat's host campus, which to me had seemed pleasant enough but not extraordinary in any way. This, I now thought, is how

Thich Nhat Hanh sees. I was suddenly hungry and eagerly ate nearly a quart of vanilla yogurt, which tasted better than the best vanilla ice cream I'd ever had. I remembered Thich Nhat Hanh telling us to chew our food until it was liquid so we could enjoy the delicate flavors of carrots and zucchini. This, I thought, is how Thich Nhat Hanh tastes.

Over the next few months, I had shorter but equally intense experiences of heightened awareness. A baseball field I crossed on the way home from the commuter train shimmered with beauty. My heart resonated so strongly with a therapy client's feelings that I thought, at first, the emotions were my own. With regular meditation, this awareness waxed. When I slackened my meditation practice, it waned.

Awareness cuts through the tangled thought processes of the rational mind and the pull of emotion by placing us in our bodies, in direct contact with our environment, *right now*. As a therapist, and in my own personal work, becoming aware has been a slow and sometimes faltering process, but it always yields a shift toward conscious choices rather than acting reflexively from unconscious attitudes and beliefs – of responding, rather than simply reacting.

There are many tools to increase awareness. They all facilitate connection between a more aware self and the world as it is, not as we hope it is or fear it will become. The tools I use most to help me become more aware include mindfulness and meditation practices from Buddhism, attunement practices from Focusing, perception-based techniques from Gestalt Therapy, and pattern recognition and interruption strategies from Spell Psychology. But photography, writing, and even motorcycling have also helped me to become more aware. Each of us finds our own path to awareness.

By clarifying our sense of ourselves, the world outside us, and our connections to it, awareness enables us to know who we are and what we need. As it increases, we find ourselves intuitively saying "yes" when we mean yes and "no" when we mean no. Awareness, regardless of the method by which it is achieved, is an essential component of awakening from the many-faceted sleep of illusion to the full and genuine lives that are our true heritage.

6. BALANCE

You can't have a light without a dark to stick it in.
- *Arlo Guthrie*

Deep Orange Marigold

Balance: Gyroscopes and personal flywheels

My first counseling psychology supervisor once remarked that every psychologist begins as a child psychologist – as a boy or girl who, to survive childhood, develops the basic skills for psychotherapy.

I've been interested in becoming a therapist since my first year in college, but until my 50s, I didn't know how I could handle the emotions of 20 or 30 people a week. Carrying people's feelings has always been an issue for me. Only after enduring sufficient difficulties in my own life did I feel that I could handle whatever might show up in my office. Then I returned to school to train as a therapist. Now, years later, achieving balance and centeredness in the midst of what can be the stormy nature of psychotherapy practice is still a work in progress. But I *have* progressed.

For several years, I tried to use the image of rocks by the seashore as a metaphor for how I wanted to be in therapy sessions – feeling the waves wash over me, yet undisturbed by their ebb and flow. But rocks, as far as we know, are inert, and I didn't want to be inert. So I looked for a better metaphor.

I wound up thinking about gyroscopes. As a kid scientist, gyroscopes fascinated me. Keep one spinning, and you can push a gyroscope in any direction and it will always right itself. As an adult struggling to stay balanced in the midst of turmoil, I imagined a gyroscope made of light, a tiny spiral galaxy spinning inside my own belly, supplying a steadying energy. The image of something inside me that can respond to – but not be uprooted by – external forces seemed to exactly fit how I wanted to be with my clients. When I have remembered this spiral galaxy gyroscope spinning inside me, I am energized by the end of the day. I think we can all use a spiral galaxy gyroscope, or something very much like it, to stabilize us, moment to moment, as we navigate life's ups and downs. We need to move where events take us, but we also need to find our way back to center.

But sometimes, an image – even a powerful one – isn't enough. To keep on keeping on through difficult times, many of us need a more powerful, more action-oriented, metaphor. We need a personal flywheel.

A flywheel is a heavy disk that rotates evenly in response to repeated applications of kinetic energy. In an automobile, the flywheel translates the jerky explosions of an internal combustion engine into vibration-free motion. A spinning disk that maintains an even flow of energy shows up in many places in the physical world. Another example is the potter's wheel, whose mass enables it to translate the craftsman's periodic kicks into the steady rotation needed to create symmetrical bowls, platters, and similar wares.

As a therapist, I often help people find their personal flywheels. By that I mean an interest or passion that is not part of a job, a chore, or something to do for friends or family, but an activity we do just for ourselves, independent of time, season, or circumstance. Even when only intermittent energy is applied, a personal flywheel keeps us going in the midst of difficulties, smoothing out the vibrations. No matter what's going on, somewhere inside us the wheel keeps spinning, spinning, and all we have to do is give it a little kick to keep it going. Then the flywheel's momentum keeps *us* going until we have a chance to catch our breath.

For the last several years, my work in photography, especially the Flower Mandalas, has been my personal flywheel. But a personal flywheel can be anything you feel passionate about. For some it is a spiritual connection and the activities associated with it, whether they are participating in a religious community or observing their own private rituals. For others, it's a physical activity – working out, doing yoga, playing a sport for the sheer joy of it. Outdoor activities such as gardening, hiking, boating, or fishing may also fill that role, as can a vast range of hobbies and avocations.

What is important is that the activity be meaningful to you and that you do it, rain or shine, whether you are tired or full of energy, giving the wheel a little kick whenever you can to keep it spinning smoothly and your balance intact.

7. CARING

Too often we underestimate the power of a touch, a smile, a kind word, a listening ear, an honest compliment, or the smallest act of caring, all of which have the potential to turn a life around.

- *Leo Buscaglia*

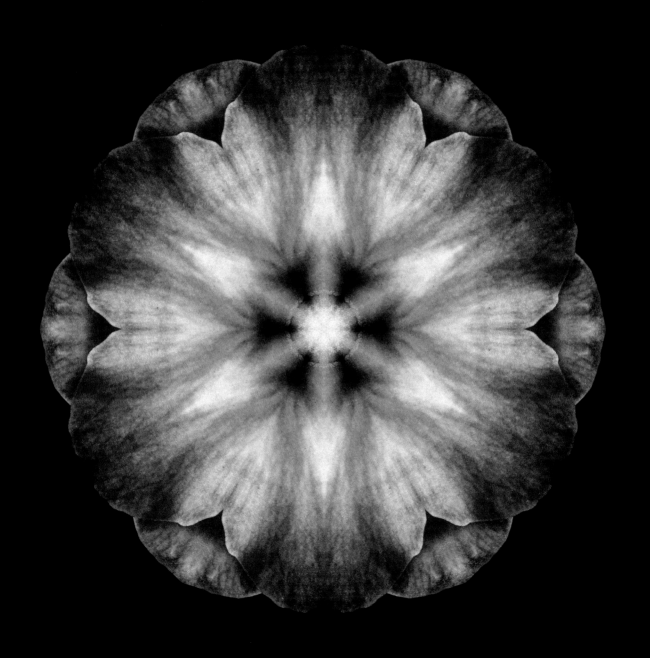

Pink and White Impatiens

CARING: THE LANGUAGES OF CARING

We all have our own ways of showing love, and these ways are also, most of the time, how we want love to be shown to us. I think of this phenomenon as our "languages of caring."

Unlike the spoken word, when it's obvious if two people are talking in different languages, we don't always know when our languages of caring are dissimilar. Because we're frequently drawn to romantic partners whose primary ways of showing love are different from ours, sometimes caring gets lost in mistranslation. The result is like what happens in the O. Henry story "The Gift of the Magi." In this tale, a young man sells his prized possession, his father's watch, to buy his wife fancy combs for her beautiful hair. The young woman, meanwhile, has sold her hair so she can buy a platinum fob chain for her husband's watch. Both try their hardest to please the other, and each sacrifices something important to do so, but in the end they have only their good intentions.

Like so many aspects of love, our languages of caring are largely products of the culture we grew up in. We learn how to show love and affection from our parents, relatives, neighbors, and friends. Some express it mainly through words, some through physical affection, others with gifts, acts of kindness, or by showing keen interest in each others' lives.

We take all this into our later relationships, and we speak to each other in the languages we learned, expecting to be spoken to the same way in return. So: A man does everything he knows how to do to show his partner how much he loves her. He works hard every day, takes care of the finances, pays for expensive family vacations, cleans up after dinner, asks about her day. But she keeps feeling that he doesn't care about her or their relationship, and as the years pass she grows increasingly resentful and distant. She still tells him daily how much she loves him and often tries to be physically affectionate, but he seems sullen and withdrawn and she can't figure out why. The problem: He shows love mainly through gifts and doing for his loved ones, while she may need loving words and caresses. And she shows love through tender words and touch, but he needs her to take an interest in the things he's passionate about. And so on, in various permutations and combinations of misconnection.

Although sometimes the caring really *is* only one-way, most people start out earnestly attempting to demonstrate their love. But when their languages differ, they miss the mark. Then each tries harder in the ways they know, much as someone might speak more loudly to a foreigner who doesn't understand the local language. Because these "louder" signals are still misinterpreted, as the cycle continues, both giver and receiver feel increasingly rejected, angry, and eventually hopeless.

By the time couples show up for counseling, many of them really *have* stopped showing they care. Each withholds from the other what they believe they haven't gotten, often recreating past experiences of deprivation, thereby subverting the emotionally corrective, co-transformative experience their relationship has the potential to be. The key to reversing this destructive cycle is becoming aware that there actually *are* differences in languages of caring, followed by willingness on both sides to learn how the other loves.

My landlords in Albany, where I lived shortly after my near-death experience, were Holocaust survivors. He was Polish, she Hungarian. At critical points in their imprisonment, he had found ways to provide her with enough food to keep her from starving to death. After their concentration camp was liberated, they left together, eventually arriving in the United States. When I met them, they both spoke English quite well, but in the camp, she spoke only Hungarian and he only Polish and Yiddish. At first they communicated through sign language and the occasional inadvertent interpreter who spoke both Hungarian and Yiddish or Polish. They knew they had to learn a common language if the relationship was to survive. And so do we, in our languages of caring, if ours are also to survive.

In practice, successful couples, once aware of differences in their languages of caring, seldom need to learn an entirely new one. Instead, each becomes increasingly fluent in the other's language, between them developing more varied ways to express their love. Even after years of misunderstanding, expressing their feelings in a shared language can reverse the erosion. Rather than breaking apart or living parallel, disconnected lives, by creating a common language, we can transcend our limitations and become not only closer to each other, but also more full versions of ourselves.

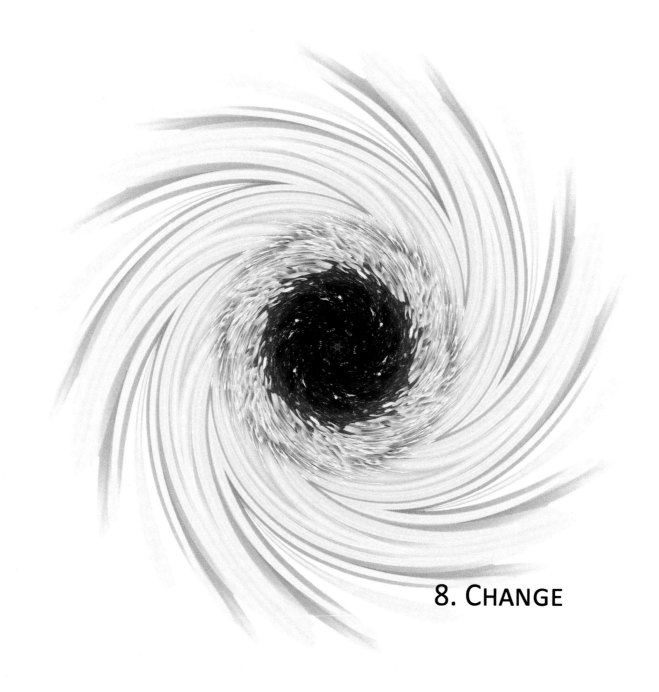

8. CHANGE

A man cannot step into the same river twice.

   - *Heraclitis of Ephesus*

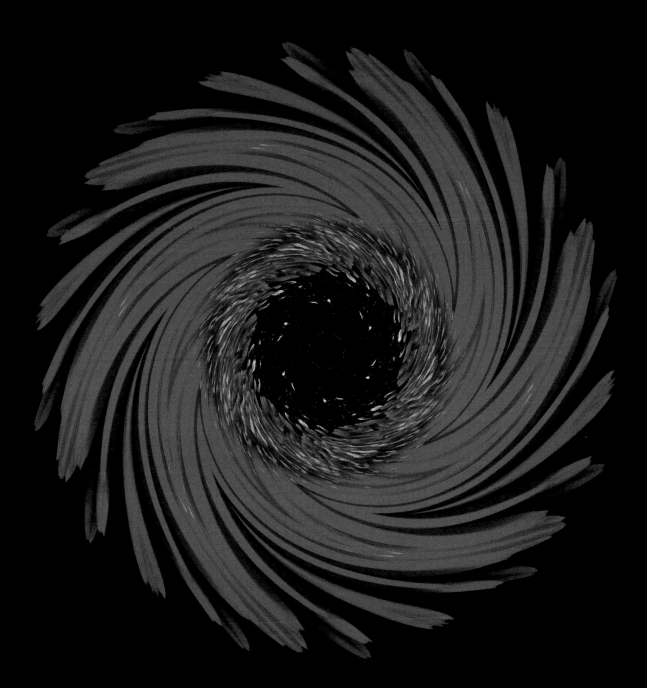

Dying Amaryllis

CHANGE: BE THE CHANGE

I came of age in the late '60s, the era of the first man on the moon, the Vietnam War, Woodstock, free love, civil rights marches, and the assassinations of iconic figures including Robert Kennedy, Martin Luther King, and Malcolm X. It was a time of reinventing the mores, values, and attitudes of the Depression-era parents who raised us. Bob Dylan's "The Times They Are a-Changin'" was our anthem – and our hope. We believed we could "change the world": end war and poverty, achieve racial equality, bring literacy to the illiterate, and recreate the Paradise from which we felt we had fallen long ago. *We* could do it. *My* generation. Us, not them.

I finished high school in 1969 and that year discovered the poetry of William Blake, Allen Ginsberg, and Robert Bly. These poet radicals became my role models. Much of my first year in college I spent attending concerts by topical protest singers, encircling draft boards, demonstrating on college campuses and in Washington, D.C. But by the time the war ended, I knew I wasn't cut out for the life of a political radical, not even a poet radical. I was still motivated to "change the world" – but how?

I became a seeker and a drifter. I briefly lived on a farm owned by an environmental design professor from the University at Buffalo who wanted to build affordable houses from indigenous materials, a project that ended when he died suddenly from a brain hemorrhage. I took a two-month motorcycle trip around the northeast and landed, eventually, in Manhattan. Still hunting for a way to "change the world," I found work there as a reporter for weekly newspapers and as a part-time art teacher at the Brooklyn Museum. For five years, I wandered New York's streets and subways, my camera, tape recorder, and notepad at the ready. I developed a writing/photography style I thought of as "slow journalism," modeled on the work of Walker Evans and James Agee's *Let Us Now Praise Famous Men* and Studs Terkel's *Working*.

I moved from documentary to fiction writing and returned to grad school, first in creative writing and later in English. During a lengthy recovery from a brush with death, my search for a way to "change the world" shifted again, toward more intimate and individual connection, and I eventually found psychotherapy. A close friend ends every email to me saying he hopes I'm still "saving the world one client at a time."

I have felt purposeful in all these things. Yet I have also mourned the loss of the vision my generation had of a different world – until, that is, a recent vacation in Germany, where I spent a few days in the former East Berlin. In my last hour there, as I looked for somewhere to have lunch, a young man with a goatee and long blonde hair grabbed my shoulder and said, "Did you go to Woodstock?"

"Me?"

"Yeah, you."

"Well, as a matter of fact I did."

Triumphantly turning to companions seated nearby, he exclaimed, "See! I told you!"

Another young man, darker complexioned, hair in a topknot and holding a beer in one hand, said, "Can I give you a hug?"

I paused, suspicious of pickpockets, then nodded. "Sure, why not?"

They were a foursome: The one who had asked me about Woodstock was Swedish, the hugger was Italian, and a young couple was from L.A. Like the majority of the people I had seen in East Berlin, they were all in their mid-20s. The young woman asked me what my most lasting impression was from Woodstock. "When I arrived at the festival and saw half a million people like me, I felt that we could change everything," I said. "But things didn't really go that way, in the end. After a generational blip, they've more or less gone back to how they were."

She shook her head. "But you *did* make a difference!" she said. She gestured around the table. "We're all continuing what you started. You're like our Founding Fathers!"

For half an hour, we talked about how my generation had influenced theirs. For the Italian, inherited change was simply to be able to drink beer on the street and dress however he wanted; for the Swede, to make and listen to whatever music he liked; for the two Americans, to do creative design and to congregate in East Berlin where, with others like themselves, they might forge their own Woodstock Nation.

That brief encounter has stayed with me. Maybe our attempt to "change the world" didn't die with the '60s after all. Maybe it *is* alive, in its own form, in the generation that succeeded us. Maybe what we planted still grows and we shall all, one day, reap its harvest.

9. CHOICE

It's choice – not chance – that determines your destiny.
- *Jean Nidetch*

White Lily

CHOICE: REPATTERNING

NOTE: The opinions expressed in the following joke do not necessarily represent those held by The Management.

So, there is this story about two lawyers. One of them walks out of a bank and sees an old lady fumbling with her purse while she tries to stay balanced on her cane. Eventually, she hobbles away. As the lawyer reaches where she was standing, he spots a $100 bill on the sidewalk. He's sure the old lady dropped it. He picks up the money and then realizes he's faced with a moral dilemma. (Beat.) Should he tell his partner?

Each of our actions and inactions defines us. And yet, though most of us understand this even as children (Santa Claus "knows if you've been bad or good, so be good for goodness sake!"), making the right choice is sometimes elusive.

Our choices are limited by our patterns, which strive to reinforce themselves. When our patterns are working well for us, that's good. But when we're stuck in a dysfunctional loop, our patterns still tirelessly reassert themselves despite our best efforts to circumvent them. According to a recent study, changing even a simple habit takes about nine months of consistent effort. Altering our more complex patterns, whether they derive from childhood coping mechanisms or cultural inheritances, is harder. The process is similar to an operating system upgrade: A lot of old code needs to be rewritten.

Although we may have little say about the cards we are dealt, the good news is that we can learn to change how we play them. Awareness is a necessary precursor to change, but it's not enough. We also need to consistently reinforce new thoughts, feelings, beliefs, and actions.

Psychotherapy is a marvelous laboratory for repatterning. Over time, I see my clients vacillate between repeating and reinventing, as they act out some old patterns and break others. Sometimes they feel as if the struggle to make better choices will never be over. Sometimes there is a breakthrough followed by consistent positive changes in how and what they choose. More often, I see a slow accretion of positive change interrupted by brief relapses into old ways of feeling, thinking, and behaving. That's how transformation seems to occur: a little here, a little there, a little forward, sometimes a little back. One choice at a time.

Momentary choices – "Should I tell my partner?" – may define us in that moment, but breaking our patterns frees up our deepest blocks and empowers us, with increasing frequency, to make choices that reflect our core selves. For this to happen, we need to tune up our psychological immune systems.

When our immune systems are working as they were designed to, they skillfully identify our own tissues as "us" and nutrients as "good for us" while simultaneously distinguishing pathogens and toxins as "not us" and "not good for us," all without conscious intervention. When our immune systems are not functioning well, they misidentify friendly substances as the enemy, and they fail to recognize the unfriendly nature of genuine threats.

A psychological immune system works the same way. And, much as repairing a damaged physical immune system requires attention to diet, exercise, and other lifestyle factors, repairing a psychological immune system also takes regular, consistent attention and effort.

To heal a damaged psychological immune system, we must believe that different choices are possible; find support for new ways of being and doing; repeat our new choices often enough to replace old habits; and acknowledge even small positive changes, so that we don't lose hope if we suffer a setback. Over time, we can develop our facility to respond to what our true natures want, need, and are striving to be. Then we can more routinely choose to say "yes" to what supports our fullest selves and "no" to what does not.

None of this is easy. I sometimes see myself reacting to triggers even though I know they *are* triggers, making questionable choices even though I know they *are* questionable, my own patterns running as efficiently as the day they came off the production floor. "I should be able to do better than this!" I tell myself. But after years of effort, I also see progress and note with pleasure that I have completely replaced some old, dysfunctional patterns with new, much-improved models. In itself, that's gratifying, and it also reminds me that other old patterns can yield, too, if only I persist.

At times I still hover at the threshold of positive change, uncertain which way to go. Yet I also continue to deeply sense parts of myself that have been waiting for a lifetime to be listened to and acted on. When these parts awaken from their slumber, the effect is as breathtaking as the sun rising on a new day.

10. COMPASSION

Until he extends the circle of his compassion to all living
things, man will not himself find peace.

   - *Albert Schweitzer*

White Daffodil

COMPASSION: FROM BOTH SIDES, NOW

During my first year of therapist training, for three days each week I commuted to Boston in heavy traffic, worked all day as an intern, attended three hours of class, and drove home, arriving there with six hours to sleep before I had to get up and do it again. It was an exhausting process and I sometimes considered giving it up.

On one late-night trek, however, I remembered a remark from a fellow classmate: "This is spiritual work we're doing, David," he said. I recalled that day's clients – earnest young art students – and was suddenly awash in a wave of fondness. Hurtling bleary-eyed through the darkness, it occurred to me that I was preparing for a career where I would be paid to love people. Or, more specifically, to be compassionate with the suffering of others and do what I could to relieve it.

Immediately preceding my therapist training, I'd had a difficult personal lesson in compassion, perhaps the most trying I have experienced, that helped prepare me for this path. A man who had befriended me for seven years, and whom I regarded as one of my closest friends, had infiltrated himself into my romantic relationship, broken it, arranged for me to discover them together, and then, a few weeks later, had discarded my former girlfriend. He had, it seemed, used her to get to me.

The effect was shattering. At first I was consumed by anguish and enduring each hour seemed more than I could bear. Then hatred, briefly empowering, took over. My body grew rigid with a boiling anger I'd never experienced: the anger of betrayal. Throughout the day, I fantasized about acts of retribution, most of them violent. I slept badly, haunted by anxious dreams, and for several months woke every night obsessively re-constructing my encounters with my former friend, searching for signs I had missed that could explain this violation. As weeks passed, I learned from others that he had a history of breaking relationships going back many years, and that he'd left a trail of bitterness and broken hearts throughout the community. For several months, I greedily took in the stories of his betrayals, now freely offered by friends and acquaintances. (News spreads quickly in a small community.) Although my vengeful fantasies, middle-of-the-night ruminations, and heated exchanging of stories

sometimes provided temporarily relief, more often they simply rehearsed and reinforced my feelings of loss, anger, and despair.

Fortunately, during this difficult time a friend introduced me to the compassion-based practice of metta. Metta is a form of meditation intended to cultivate loving kindness. The practice consists of a wish for something positive for yourself, for someone you love, for someone you know casually, for someone with whom you are having difficulty, and finally, for all sentient beings.

Positive thoughts for myself, my loved ones, acquaintances, and for all sentient beings came to me with relative ease, and over time they brought a subtle sense of peace. Wishing anything positive toward the people with whom I was having the greatest difficulty, my former friend and former partner, was much more challenging. To go from hatred and betrayal to loving kindness seemed impossible.

With persistent encouragement from a Buddhist therapist to continue the practice, however, I was eventually able to see that, although I was still consumed with hatred, I no longer wished my former friend an agonizing, premature death, and I no longer wished my former girlfriend a barren existence. As I continued to practice metta, I found myself gradually wishing more positive forms of loving kindness. Little by little, I began to experience a liberating acceptance, and to view both of them not as trusted companions and confidants who had intentionally betrayed me, but as people who had themselves been injured in different ways and who were merely acting out the consequences of that harm.

By the time a year or so had passed, I had forgiven my partner and felt no anger toward my former friend. For her, I wished only happiness and a fulfilling life, and for him, that he would become conscious of his destructive patterns and bring them to a halt. For myself, I felt gratitude for the practice that had served me so well and hoped I would continue it.

Compassion is neither naive nor weak. Feeling it didn't significantly alter my actions: I still lived the life I would otherwise have lived. But it healed me from the continual wounding of hate.

11. CONNECTION

Only connect!
- *E.M. Forster*

Red and Yellow Marigold

Connection: Metamorphosis

I am a person with a big heart and a deep need to be connected, but I grew up alienated and insulated from others and myself. The arc of my life has been to move from disconnection to connectedness, both internally and with the world outside.

I am what I now understand to be a "highly sensitive person" – someone who takes in, on both a sensory and emotional level, more than most people do. There are a lot of us – some 20% of the population, according to Elaine Aron, author of *The Highly Sensitive Person* and originator of the term. It's a blessing and a curse: We can't screen much out, but we also have more data available at a conscious level.

When I was growing up in the '50s, nobody knew about highly sensitive people. I was a stranger in the strange land of my family, neighborhood, and school. The noisy, gregarious world was too much for me, and it frequently informed me that I was also not right – "too sensitive" and "too shy" – for it. So I retreated into another, more manageable one.

The launch of the Soviet satellite Sputnik drew me to science. I became part of the generation who would not let the Russians beat us in the space race. In my bedroom, I hung posters of all the Soviet and American rockets and satellites. I wanted to be a rocket scientist and, perhaps, also an astronaut, but rocket science was a long way off when I was 7. In the meantime, I became increasingly preoccupied with the workings of both the natural and technological worlds. By age 10, I was also consuming vast amounts of science fiction. I identified most with the stories of mutants and superheroes, whose differences at first made them outcasts but later the saviors of mankind.

Connection was so difficult for me that I seldom attempted it. At home, I kept out of the way, secreted in my basement laboratory until one experiment backfired and choked my father with chlorine gas, banishing me and my scientific investigations to the garage. My connections with the few neighborhood and school friends I had were limited to our common interests in comic books, science, and science fiction.

I remained in this isolated state until my second year in high school, when moving to a larger house landed me in a new school district. This relocation launched a process of expansion that changed everything.

I came out of invisibility. I awoke to the Vietnam War and become a high school radical, collaborating with some of my classmates on a left-wing magazine we called *Cynic*. I discovered love and sex. I applied to engineering schools, but by the time I left for Cornell, I'd experienced Woodstock and knew, deep down, that I no longer wanted to be a NASA engineer.

Over the next decade, I developed the less analytical, more expansive parts of myself. In college, I did just enough to get by in engineering classes, and threw myself into literature, psychology, and writing. I turned on to marijuana and LSD, radical politics, Eastern religion, protest songs, and rock and roll. I transferred to the University at Buffalo, where I became an English major and also volunteered at a mental hospital and a parent-run free school. I learned how to start conversations and make people laugh. I hitchhiked across the U.S. and back through Canada to force myself to connect, if only for a lift to the next town or to find somewhere to crash for the night.

After college, I landed in Manhattan, where the drive to connect led me to write stories and take pictures for weekly newspapers. Reporting forced me to interview strangers, while the camera provided a place to retreat to, if that level of contact felt too intense. I taught children, and found new, more playful parts of myself emerging.

My near-death experience took connecting to a new level. Afterwards, many of the left-brain functions I'd excelled at were more difficult, while right-brain equivalents replaced them. I couldn't feel my way into machines anymore, but I could directly experience the emotions of others. I stepped up my spiritual quest, looking more deeply into near-death studies, Buddhism, and Sufism, and working with psychotherapists, eventually choosing to become both Buddhist and therapist myself.

One friend referred to me as "jumping around like a cockroach" until I became a therapist, but I see my history differently: as seeking progressively deeper ways to connect. Though I still have a way to go, I have come nearly 180 degrees from my childhood of hiding.

Many of my clients also struggle with connection. Often, I can lead by example, assuring them that, with a little help and some diligence, they can get there, too.

12. COURAGE

Man cannot discover new oceans unless he has the
courage to lose sight of the shore.

- *André Gide*

Red Lily

COURAGE: THE HERO'S JOURNEY

There are many forms of courage. Physical courage enables us to face danger and perform daring feats of strength and agility. The courage to defy convention lets us dance, as Henry David Thoreau put it, to the beat of our own drummer. And there is moral courage, which moves us to sacrifice even our lives for freedom, justice, and other causes if we believe in them strongly enough.

In my own life and in those of my clients, the most profound form of courage is the willingness to face deeply entrenched fears and self-limiting beliefs and to move beyond them: to see obstacles not as roadblocks but as opportunities for growth. This is how we transition from surviving to thriving, victim to victor.

As a therapist, I see remarkable displays of courage: Coming back from a suicide attempt and finding purpose as a healer. Overcoming addiction and becoming an artist. Ending a marriage, or recommitting to one. Breaking free of crippling phobias and isolating depressions. Risking rejection by setting boundaries or by asking for what one truly needs. Giving up a lucrative but stultifying job to pursue a passion. And many more. It is the most gratifying part of my job.

The model for courage I use in my own life and with many of my clients is that of the Hero's Journey, as delineated in Joseph Campbell's landmark book *The Hero With a Thousand Faces*. This comprehensive study sifts through the hero stories of a vast range of cultures and time periods and identifies a structure common to almost all of them, still present in most of the action dramas and even the comedies of today. They are the stories of the not-quite hero, sometimes the not-at-all hero, who, through an unwanted adventure, blossoms into true heroism.

In each of these tales, the protagonist appears to be living a passable life, but beneath the surface there is a flaw. Early in the story, he is thrust into situations where this hidden flaw is revealed. Things go topsy-turvy: Friends may become enemies, enemies friends, and the rules the protagonist has lived by no longer seem to apply. He sinks into increasingly difficult circumstances, encountering one obstacle after another, until he hits bottom. This is the decisive moment. There he will remain, a failed hero, unless he finds the courage to rise back up.

If he does rise, his return to the world he knew is as fraught with peril as was his trip down, but now he knows what he's fighting for. Again he encounters obstacle after obstacle, but this time, his challenges make him more determined. At last, he arrives home, more fully revealed and with something to offer that he could not have given before. As Campbell put it, "The hero comes back… with the power to bestow boons on his fellow man."

The common denominator for all these stories, whether they are mythological epics like the *Odyssey* or present-day films like the *Star Wars* series, is that the protagonist, through finding the courage to rise from defeat, each time grows a little wiser, a bit more skillful, and acquires greater inner strength. Even when he doesn't survive the final battle, he dies a hero.

In difficult times, I deliberately expose myself to tales of heroism. For inspiration, I watch films like *Cinderella Man* or *The Matrix*, or I revisit sections of the *Odyssey*, to strengthen my resolve to get up from the mat, to wake from the sleep of Circe, and to move ahead. When I am trying to inspire clients who are at the bottom of their Hero's Journey arc, I often ask who their heroes are and explore the qualities that make them heroic. I point out to my clients that they have selected these men and women because something in their own nature resonates with these qualities. Our work together brings out the clients' heroism so they can continue their personal journeys.

The difference between those who successfully reach the end of their Hero's Journeys and those who do not isn't better opportunities, more strength, or superior allies, but the courage to get up and try again, even when the odds seem insurmountable and discouragement feels overwhelming. When we follow this simple precept, we grow from our struggles and, regardless of the external outcome, acquire stature and nobility that cannot be taken away.

13. CURIOSITY

Curiosity is lying in wait for every secret.
  - *Ralph Waldo Emerson*

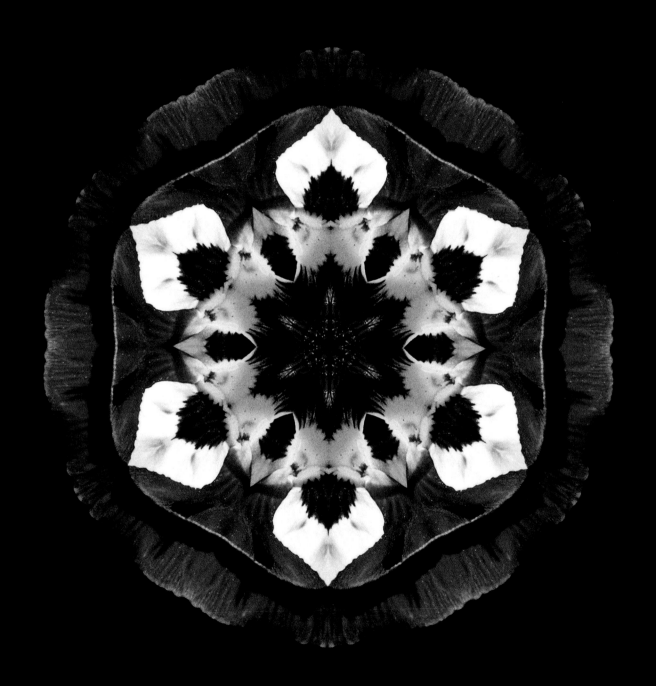

Purple Pansy

CURIOSITY: REVIVING THE CAT

In all my years of formal education, from elementary through graduate schools, no teacher ever suggested that I pay attention to curiosity. Not one, not even once. Instead, I learned that "curiosity killed the cat."

Following my curiosity has always been an extra-curricular activity, but it's the driving force for almost everything I've done, from childhood to the present. This book is itself the result of curiosity. While experimenting with new software, I wondered what would happen if I applied a kaleidoscope effect to a picture of a flower, already kaleidoscopic. The result was my first Flower Mandala, the Dandelion Head that accompanies the essay "Acceptance."

Curiosity is among our most vital emotions. It's how we discover what is important about ourselves, others, and the world. All the journalistic prompts – Who? What? When? Where? Why? How? – are expressions of curiosity; without them there would be no news. And it is no accident that the Mars Science Lab gathering data on the Red Planet is named "Curiosity."

According to Thomas Kuhn, in *The Structure of Scientific Revolutions*, scientific progress is driven by paradigm-shifters who get curious about anomalies and challenge the status quo. Does this current theory, the paradigm shifters ask, explain all our data, or is there something that doesn't fit? Paradigm shifts turn previous theories on their heads, leading to broader, deeper, and more encompassing understandings. Without new paradigms – and the curiosity about anomalies that drives their discovery – what we think of as civilization could not have come into being.

As a therapist, I pay attention to curiosity. A client has repeated the same thing three times this session: Did I miss something important? Does she feel I have not heard her? Or I sense that something he's saying seems a little off: Is there more? Is something hidden? Or there's a little laugh, a tilting of the head to one side, then the client closes her eyes for a moment: Where did she go, just then?

Paying attention to my own curiosity can enrich a session, but when clients themselves get curious, transformation follows. When a client says "I was angry," then checks those words against a bodily awareness of what he or she feels, and then realizes, "No, actually, I was *hurt*," a paradigm is shifting.

The combined curiosity of therapist and client often elicits the greatest changes. For example, a client recovering from a destructive relationship was interested in dating again, but his strategy was limited to going to bars with his friends and trying pickup lines. I got curious. "How's that working out?" I asked. "Not well," he admitted.

I suggested using curiosity as a more genuine way to get a conversation going and proposed, as practice, that he start one with me. "Ask me something or tell me something," I said.

He noticed a poster of my mandala images hanging over my desk. "So, did you make that?" he asked.

"Yes, I did," I said. I pointed to the pictures on the opposite wall. "I made those, too."

That was his pickup line. He was quiet for a moment, then shrugged. Nothing more to say.

"Are you actually curious about art?" I asked. "Because I've never heard you talk about it."

"Not really."

"Okay, then try again, but this time ask me something you really *are* curious about."

He glanced around the room. "Did you get that lamp at IKEA?"

"I did," I said. "Almost everything here is from IKEA." I told him my story of squeezing a roomful of office furniture into a friend's RAV4. He shared his of furnishing his first apartment completely from IKEA. We talked about our mutual frustration with IKEA's wordless assembly instructions. Soon we were in a natural back-and-forth conversation that quickly went beyond IKEA.

It's often hard to pinpoint the precise catalyst for transformation, but that conversation seemed to be a turning point for this client. Not long afterward, he found a new girlfriend, got a better job, and bought a condo in a new town. He also resumed old hobbies and took up new activities he'd always wanted to try. By tapping into his curiosity about IKEA, not only did he learn how to go beyond a pickup line, he also became curious about who he was and how he wanted to live.

Without curiosity, we are left unaware, unexcited, unoriginal, unalive. With it, we have a chance to thrive, not only as individuals, but as a species. In a color-inside-the-lines world, the curious cat does sometimes get killed. But in the great world outside those lines, the curious cat is king.

14. DESIRE

You are what your deep, driving desire is. As your deep,
driving desire is, so is your will. As your will is, so is
your deed. As your deed is, so is your destiny.

   - Brihadaranyaka Upanishad

Yellow and Orange Sunflower

DESIRE: EMPOWERING "YES" AND "NO"

Poet Stanley Kunitz asks, "What makes the engine go?" His answer: "Desire, desire, desire."

Desire motivates us to find food when we're hungry, drink when we're dry, seek warmth when we're chilly, sleep when we're tired, make friends when we're lonely. When our basic survival needs are satisfied, our desires moves further up what psychologist Abraham Maslow called the "hierarchy of needs," and we look for safety, love, and belonging. At the top of the pyramid is self-actualization – the desire to become the fullest versions of ourselves.

Movement up the hierarchy of needs is our natural tendency, but it's often interrupted. For people living in great poverty, even the basic desires for survival needs can't be satisfied. For many others, desires further up the hierarchy are thwarted by our early conditioning.

Kurt Vonnegut's short story "Harrison Bergeron" takes the suppression of desire to a societal extreme. In his dystopian future, people are made "equal" by handicapping anyone who is superior to the least of its citizens in any way. The Handicapper General enforces this "equality" by legislating and enforcing handicaps – ugly masks for the too beautiful, earphones that emit deafening sounds for the too smart, and heavy weights for anyone faster or stronger than the slowest and the weakest. The protagonist is Harrison Bergeron, a 14-year-old boy who wears the most severe handicaps ever issued. As the story progresses, he meets a similarly encumbered young woman. Defiantly, they cast off their handicaps and dance, rising 30 feet into the air, where they kiss. It is a spellbinding moment – that abruptly ends when the Handicapper General herself shoots them down on national television.

In Vonnegut's futuristic nightmare, it is mechanical handicaps that society imposes, but his story, like most science fiction, is an allegory for today. We have no Handicapper General, but many of us go through our lives saying "yes" when our desires beg us to say "no," and "no" when they cry out for "yes."

Instead of our families, schools, and culture encouraging our genuine desires, we are led to desire what others want us to want. When asked "What do you want to be when you grow up?" what child answers, "I'd like to sell insurance" or "I'd like to work in a factory" or "I'd like to sit in a cubicle all day" or "I'd like to fight in a war half a world away"? As Rodgers and Hammerstein so eloquently put it, to want these things, "you've got to be carefully taught."

Early on, we learn the right words, such as responsibility and respect, but the wrong definitions: "responsibility" becomes "obligation" and "respect" becomes "obedience." Conditional love is one of our most insidious teachers: "We will love you if we approve of you. We will love you if you do what we want you to do. We will love you if you fulfill *our* desires."

When we suppress our real desires, we replace them with cravings for approval, success, power, and for goods and services created mainly for profit. Instead of self-actualizing, we get stuck feeding a hunger that can't be satisfied because it doesn't yearn for what we desire, only for what we've been conditioned to want. Like addictions, our pseudo-desires keep us from being who we are meant to be and doing what we are meant to do.

So how do we get out of this mess? The answer: One discernment at a time, we retrain ourselves to connect with the source of our desires.

An exercise: Imagine that inside you is a little child you care for very much. As you go through your day, imagine asking him or her, "Do you like that? Or would you rather have something else?" Don't answer with your conscious mind. Instead, wait for a sensation within you to signal "yes," "no," or "something else."

The place that answers is where your desires live. Sensing, and then acting on, these real desires encourages empowered decisions. The more we make decisions that reflect our true desires, the more cravings, envy, and even shame, guilt, and confusion diminish. Rather than being bounced from one pseudo-desire's urgings to the next, we move through life with increasing confidence and inner security.

What would our world be like if we were all empowered to follow our true desires? Would some of us still work unsatisfying jobs, be in unsatisfying relationships, act out of guilt or obligation, hatred or fear? Would we continue to trade the dreams of our youth, the things we are passionate about, for trinkets? Or would we do only what satisfies the essential needs of ourselves and others, freeing the rest of our time, energy, and resources for fulfilling our higher desires?

I hope we all get a chance to find out.

15. DREAMS

Keep true to the dreams of thy youth.
  - *Herman Melville*

Pink and White Hibiscus Moscheutos

DREAMS: NOT GONE, NOT FORGOTTEN

Clients often come for therapy with the uneasy sense that something is stuck. They have stumbled into marriages, occupations, places, ways of life that are off, and the architecture of their lives feels misshapen. Because I have also had the experience of a misshapen life, I pay attention.

Many of us enter adulthood not as single, unified wholes, but as tripartite beings. One part is nurtured by the environment and sprouts and grows, like a seed that gets the right amount of water, nutrients, and light. Another, rejected by the environment, goes dormant. A third, better able to withstand this unwelcoming environment, displaces the dormant part, like a weed taking over a patch of garden. It becomes a false self that helps us cope with the sometimes difficult conditions we find ourselves in as children.

A personal example: As a boy, my scientific/mathematical part was encouraged by my environment. It earned me good grades and occasional praise from my parents. The emotionally sensitive and artistically gifted part was largely ignored. It went underground, and depression and isolation rose to take its place. I carried this false self with me to college, where, in the tumult at the end of the '60s, the dormant part began to stir.

I first encountered the phrase "Keep true to the dreams of thy youth" in a college literature class, where I learned that Herman Melville had taped it to his desk. The next summer, I hitchhiked across the United States to find out what *my* dreams were. I returned to Buffalo four months later with a list of missing pieces. On it were writing, photography, woodworking, meditation, and, to carry on the traveler's sense of adventure, motorcycling. The list became the curriculum of a program to complete myself, and self-actualization became my dream. I pursued it for about 10 years, until I severely injured my back just before starting a master's program in creative writing.

Melville's professional writing career came to a halt following scathing criticism of *Moby Dick*. He entered a personal Dark Age, working as a customs inspector for 19 years, during which he was virtually silent as a novelist. He was 66 when he finally retired from the customs house and wrote *Billy Budd*, arguably the best short novel ever written in English.

On a smaller scale, my back injury, combined with relentless criticism from the director of my writing program and continuing rejection by my father for leaving engineering school, halted what appeared to be a promising writing career. I limped through the writing program, took a crash course in computer science, and found work as a software technical writer, a position that satisfied neither my father's wish for me to be an engineer nor my own to succeed as a creative writer. In this, my Dark Age, writing, photography, serious reading, motorcycling, meditation, and working with my hands all stopped. A familiar false self arose to fill the vacancies and disconnected me from my dreams. But throughout this dark period, I had Melville's phrase taped to my computer monitor, and its subtle insistence helped keep my dreams alive.

Remembering the dreams of our youth can loosen the grip of the false self. Reactivating them can reshape a misshapen life, permitting the suppressed part to resurface and take its rightful place within our being. Remembering my dreams about writing helped lever me out of corporations and into graduate school, an environment more friendly to my creative self. Then other things started coming back: reading, photography, meditation, and even motorcycling. Each rekindled dream has restored me, like a wilted garden springing up after a summer rain, enabling me to enact a previously unrealized dream of becoming a psychotherapist.

Reactivating dreams can happen at any age. In my therapy practice, I come upon many people in their 20s and 30s who already think it's too late for them. We work together to remember their dreams. Sometimes, I can save them 10 or 20 years of slumber.

Many of us have rekindled dreams, and we can serve as models. Some examples: A client who wanted to be an attorney before she knew the word "attorney" finished law school. A few years ago, a friend retired from medicine and has since become an award-winning photographer. Another friend found her way back to music and languages after 30 years in the finance industry. One of my brothers, a highly successful business man, completed his college education at 58.

None of us has the nine lives of the proverbial cat, but we *can* fully exploit this one's possibilities by remembering the dreams of our youth and using them as a beacon to show us who we really are and what we can look forward to becoming.

16. FAILURE

Never confuse a single defeat with a final defeat.
 - *F. Scott Fitzgerald*

Purple Iris

FAILURE: OPTIONS

In our success-driven culture, there seems to be no end of helpful adages for dealing with failure. But "failure is not an option" is small comfort to those who believe they have already failed, "if at first you don't succeed, try, try again" seldom encourages the already discouraged, and "we learn more from failure than from success" is scant consolation when we don't see a silver lining in the cloud of our defeats.

The problem with these guidelines is that the underlying concept of "failure" is flawed. Most of us hope we will achieve what we strive for and believe that when we don't, we have failed. Striving for what we want is a natural part of our makeup, but attachment to the outcome of those strivings can imprison us.

For a young client whose motto was "Number 2 is the first loser," success meant being the best at anything he tried. The pressure of being Number 1 was constant and he lived in a nightmare of fear that someone, somewhere, was better than he was. He *was* good at what he did, but he also became the most "successful" drug abuser I've encountered. Losing his fear of failing to meet an impossible standard was his first step toward recovery.

In my own life, as a boy, taking failure off the table made me valedictorian of my high school at the expense of a lopsided life. As an adult, never giving up kept me in doomed relationships and unsatisfying occupations. When things fell apart, the "lessons" of failure did nothing to avert despair. Only by abandoning these guidelines have I been able to find freedom.

I wonder even about inspirational tales of success. Thomas Edison, when asked about his relentless attempts to find a viable filament for an incandescent light bulb, remarked, "I haven't failed. I've just found 10,000 ways that won't work." We have all benefited from Edison's persistence. But what might he have discovered had he given up his quest for the incandescent light bulb and looked for another way to turn electricity into illumination?

When we lose attachment to outcome, everything that happens just *is*. If things don't work out as we hope they will, there is no failure; our lives have simply taken a different turn. Finding ourselves on an unexpected path, we can stop and look around and ask what we can do now.

Perhaps we reevaluate, learn from our mistakes, and try, try again. Or maybe we find that one door closes, another opens, and we go through that second door instead.

Understanding the opportunities implicit in failing came to me most clearly on the day of my near-death experience. That afternoon, I was cranky and irritable, annoyed with the nurses and my girlfriend because of the inconvenience of being in the hospital, away from everything that seemed vitally important to achieving success as a college professor and novelist. A couple of hours later, however, I was fighting not to succeed but to stay alive. From that event forward, I was on a different path. Would my life have been more "successful" if I had written that novel and completed that PhD? Or has the range of experiences since then been enriching in ways that could not have occurred if I'd succeeded in achieving my original goals?

Sometimes I use *Flatland*, a short novel written by Edwin Abbot at the end of the 19th century, to help clients envision alternate selves who, rather than succumbing to defeat or rising to try again, can choose a different path. On Flatland, the inhabitants are all two-dimensional shapes. Women are triangles and men are polygons with four or more sides. These unusual beings move about on the surface of their flattened world seeing only length and width. Because they cannot view each other from above or below, the Flatlanders perceive themselves not as the shapes familiar to us from geometry, but as lines of varying lengths.

Flatland's protagonist is a Square. When a Sphere drops into his plane of existence and briefly plucks him out of Flatland, he becomes aware that although he *experiences* his world as two-dimensional, it, too, has a third dimension, the dimension of height. His mind opens.

These days, I feel a lot like the liberated Square, whose viewpoint was once limited to two dimensions but who can now sense an additional one: the dimension of possibility. When we add that dimension, we can all turn "failure" into an opportunity to explore a reality that could not have come into being, had there been "success." The trick is to be willing to say, "I thought I was going *there*, but now I'm *here*," and then to ask, "What is happening *here*?"

17. FAITH

You can do very little with faith, but you can do nothing without it.

  - *Samuel Butler*

Rhododendron 'Ponticum Roseum'

FAITH: PAYING IT FORWARD

A mentor once told me that he believed I started out as a person of great faith who had lost it early on. I've spent a long time thinking about his observation.

Faith in a divinity has always been problematic for me. The closest I have come – an understanding I arrived at when I was 10 – is that aspects of the known universe seem impossible to attribute to cosmic evolution alone. But despite decades of pondering, what was mysterious to me 50-plus years ago remains a mystery, and I continue to be agnostic. On the human scale, however, I think my mentor was on to something. On the human scale, faith is something I *have* lost, and have also found again.

The most difficult faith to recover has been faith in myself. For most of my life, an inner critic has persistently tried to convince me that I have little worth. Occasionally it has been mercifully silent, sometimes merely an annoyance, but whenever I've undertaken anything significant – a creative project, a difficult technical task, a new relationship or business venture – it uses everything in its arsenal to try to stop me, and I have to use everything in mine to persevere. What the critic is trying to do is keep me small. That's often what inner critics do.

Though they seem hurtful and self-sabotaging, inner critics usually start out as protectors. In my case, I grew up with a critical father and an angry mother. The unconscious strategy I developed to avoid hurt and humiliation was to become so tiny and innocuous that I would hardly be noticed, and therefore become a smaller target. I was quiet, withdrawn, even physically small; today, I might have been diagnosed with anorexia and depression. Being small didn't always keep me out of harm's way, but it was the best I could do at the time. To keep myself small, I created an inner critic to monitor my actions.

Well-intentioned but outmoded, my inner critic still tries to keep me small, even though I am decades away from those childhood dangers. To go forward in spite of the critic's protective harangue requires faith in myself and in the value of what I do. To feel that kind of faith, I, like most of us, needed to experience the faith that someone else had in me.

I first realized this some years ago, at a reading by Sebastian Junger from his book *The Perfect Storm*. In his introductory remarks, Junger thanked his father for always cheering him on and for encouraging him to stick with projects when he was discouraged or uncertain. At the time, my writing voice was still and my inner critic ruled. "Nothing you do will amount to anything," it said.

During the reading, I wondered what I might have accomplished as a writer, had I been supported by my father, as Junger was, and had never created this inner protector. A thoughtful and dedicated therapist I started seeing shortly afterward became that supportive father figure. By consistently reflecting back his own faith in me, he taught me to have faith in myself and, eventually, to control my inner critic.

When I decided to become a therapist myself, I recognized that many people do not have a supportive figure in their lives, and that I had the capacity to be that person not only for myself, but also for others. Early in my training, I meditated on the relationship I wanted to have with my future clients. The phrase that came to me was "true companion," someone willing to stand by his clients and accompany them wherever their lives took them, never losing sight of who they were, always reflecting back to them the light of their essential selves. From the start, I have endeavored to be that kind of therapist. I've had many clients look to me, in their darkness, for a little light, and I have assured them that my faith has not wavered, and that others, too, will come to see their light as long as they continue to make the effort to let it shine.

When I am at a temporary loss for how else to help someone, I remember that this kind of faith is more important than any therapeutic technique or intervention, and that it, alone, is often sufficient to carry someone through, as I myself was carried through by my own therapist's faith in me. Having experienced the instillation of faith, I can now pay it forward, perhaps to be paid forward again and again as the people I support go forth as fuller versions of themselves, their faith in themselves restored and their inner critics vanquished.

18. FEAR

The only thing we have to fear is fear itself.
 - *Franklin D. Roosevelt*

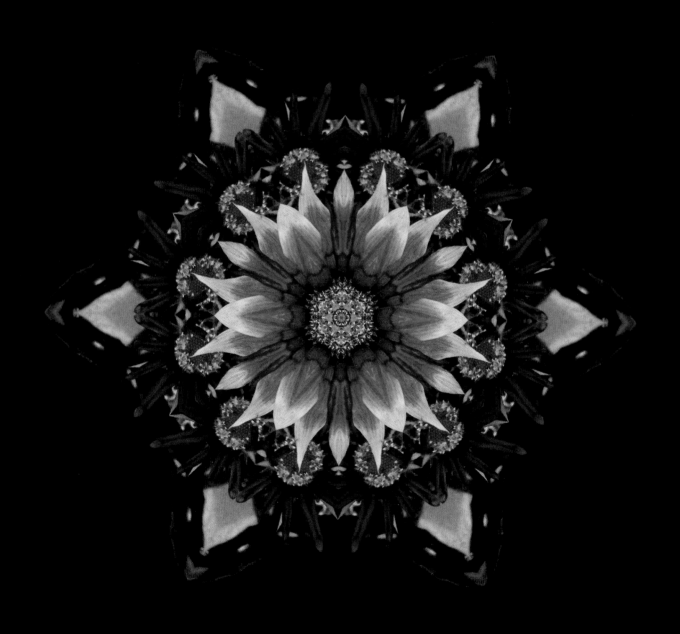

Orange Gazania

FEAR: MOVING ON

Most of us learned to be afraid before we could tell real from imagined danger. Consequently, sometimes, like a faulty check-engine light, our fight/flight/freeze mechanism is triggered in situations it wasn't designed for. Then, we may react to imagined peril and fail to respond to real threats. To recalibrate our fear monitors, we need to update our programming.

A couple summers ago, I had an opportunity to re-tune my own monitors and, in the process, discovered a new way not only to understand fear, but also to transform it.

Motorcycling was an important part of my identity throughout my 20s, but after a serious back injury in 1979, I gave it up. The injury eventually healed, and each spring I'd long to join other motorcyclists as they gracefully negotiated the back roads, but I continued to stay away. At a family event, I mentioned my longing to ride again. "Well, Dave," my brother Paul said, "I've got a motorcycle you can have, if you come and get it."

The following spring, I read two books on motorcycle safety and bought a helmet and a bus ticket to Syracuse, NY. I gave myself two days to re-learn motorcycling and another two for the trip home. I figured I'd either pick up riding right away, or I'd give up the idea for good. Either way, I'd be freed from longing.

At 6 a.m. on my first riding day, Paul and I headed to a nearby parking lot. Fear hit me like a rogue wave as soon as I got on the bike, and I was drenched in sweat before we reached our destination five long minutes later. Once there, I screeched tires on downshifts, stalled on braking, took turns too wide, overshot stop lines – errors that would get me killed in highway traffic. An inner voice kept shouting, "Don't be stupid. Give up. You'll never make it home."

After 20 minutes, I parked the bike, pulled off my helmet, and told Paul, "I don't think I can do this."

"Looked like you were doing okay to me," he said.

We talked and soon realized that both of us often felt like quitting just at the verge of success. "Mom's like that," I said. "And Dad never liked taking chances," Paul added. We hadn't grown up with a model for moving through fear; instead, we'd been taught to avoid it. But

what I had learned I could *un*learn. I still had two days and nothing to lose by trying. So I got back on the bike.

As I rode, the fear was undiminished, but the nagging voice quieted. Soon I was whipping around the parking lot at a bone-jarring 25mph. Apprehensively, I turned onto the highway and inched the speedometer up to 40. "I'm right with you," Paul shouted. A couple of miles later, he veered off to work. I spent the next few hours riding up and down a seldom-used roadway, stalling out at stop signs, struggling through U-turns, briefly panicking when I thought I'd run out of gas. But by the time Paul came home that evening, I was comfortable doing 50.

From that parking lot crisis forward, I noticed that although each new challenge was as scary as the last, what had previously been terrifying wasn't scary, anymore. The fear *seemed* the same, but I was actually making progress, and I realized I would continue to do so, as long as I kept on riding. By the end of the second day, I was as ready as I'd ever be for the 350 mile trip home.

That ride was white-knuckle all the way. I hit wet roads, grooved pavement, railroad tracks that forced me into oncoming traffic, drivers who seemed intent on killing me. I had many mini-therapy sessions at 60mph between my adult self and the panic-stricken child within. "We can do this," I would say. Rain and wind came and went, at its worst just as I reached the trickiest stretch of highway. "We're almost there," I told my child self, "we can't die now!"

In the '70s, my brothers and I used to talk about riding together, but we never pulled it off. That September, I returned to Syracuse, where, at last, we went on a group ride together. And it was great.

This battle with fear yielded several boons. Expected was regaining the thrill and sense of gracefulness I'd always gotten from motorcycling. Unexpected was a deeper connection with my brothers; we ride together as often as we can. Most surprising were the lessons I learned about overcoming fear, which I have since been able to model.

"That's badass," one of my clients remarked, after I told her I'd returned to motorcycling.

"Yeah," I said with a wink and a smile, "I guess I've still got a little badass left in me…. And so do you!"

19. FORGIVENESS

Without forgiveness, there is no future.

   - Desmond Tutu

White Daisy

FORGIVENESS: TO FORGIVE, DIVINE

Forgiveness liberates. It relieves us of guilt, shame, resentment, hatred, and feelings of victimization. Yet, according to a Gallup poll, although 95% of us recognize the need for it, 85% also have trouble forgiving. So what makes forgiveness so difficult?

Some obstacles are easy to understand. Forgiveness is hardest when harm is ongoing. Before we can offer forgiveness, we must be protected, and before we can ask to be forgiven, we must stop doing harm. Forgiveness is also challenging when injuries haven't healed. Sometimes, unhealed wounds can lock us into a pattern of attracting others who hurt us again, or they imprison us in self-protection that allows nothing healing to get through, increasing the difficulty of forgiving.

For many of us, however, the chief impediment to forgiveness is unwillingness. Our culture glorifies an "eye for an eye and a tooth for a tooth" tradition that spans millennia. Forgiveness – forgiving others, seeking forgiveness, forgiving ourselves – is seen as weakness. If we have been harmed, we may feel, we *should* punish those who hurt us, and if we cannot, we should punish them in our hearts. Releasing ourselves from these familiar, vengeful emotions through forgiveness may seem unfamiliar and unsafe.

When couples hold onto hurt and anger, there has often been a breach of trust: a rejection, an affair, some other form of betrayal. Similar patterns occur in families affected by addiction, with addict and family members alike entangled in a mutually punishing purgatory. Unforgiven wounds from childhood also fracture families, subtly re-harming both the wounded and the ones who did the original wounding.

There are multiple paths to forgiveness.

Sometimes, a sincere apology and removal of the possibility of further harm is sufficient. When I visited, in prison, one of the medical malpractice attorneys who had robbed me of my award, he seemed glad I'd come. He said he was grateful to have the opportunity to "unburden myself of guilt," even though I was one of the chief witnesses against him. We talked for a long time. Without quite saying so, I knew he was asking for forgiveness, and without quite saying so, I gave it to him.

Forgiveness comes most easily when a sincere apology is followed by diligent and sensitive efforts to make amends. So, an affair is confessed and regretted, followed by a reassuring change in behavior that withstands the test of time.

Or an addiction is admitted, the addict seeks treatment, and he or she makes consistent efforts to restore trust. Or neglect and abuse are atoned for and a new, more fulfilling relationship is attempted. From these actions, forgiveness can often spring, and from forgiveness, reconciliation.

Even in the absence of apology and amends, forgiveness can sometimes still be granted. Recognizing that we have recovered from our injuries and are now whole begins the process. Forgiving my father began with a dream I had several years after his death and concluded when I realized, finally, that I was no longer afflicted by what had been damaging in our relationship. I could then regard him with compassion, understand how his difficulties and limitations had shaped him, and forgive him for his part in our lifelong estrangement – and myself, for mine.

Similarly, it's possible to ask forgiveness from those we have harmed even when offering an apology and making amends can't occur. A decade ago, a close friend committed suicide. I was haunted by guilt over avoiding him in what turned out to be his final months. Later, I was able to see that, had our positions been reversed, I would not have wanted him to feel any responsibility for my death. I asked for his forgiveness, and in a surge of grief and tears I felt released from the burden I had been carrying.

Forgiveness can transcend relationships, freeing us not only from current injuries, but also from older, deeper ones. I see this phenomenon in couples, who often recreate in each other the childhood wounds they carry, as if they have come together to reenact old stories, but with different endings. When each finds a way to forgive the other, they can undo not only the hurt from their relationship, but also heal the damaged parts each has brought into it.

The most helpful tool I've encountered for fostering forgiveness is a Buddhist meditation.[1] It instructs us first to feel the pain of keeping our hearts closed and then offers gentle steps for opening them enough to ask forgiveness from those we have harmed, to forgive ourselves, and to forgive those who have harmed us. Cautioning that forgiveness may come slowly and cannot be forced, the meditation encourages a gradual letting go of the burdens of unforgiven acts, with each iteration lightening our load just a little, like a sigh of relief.

---

[1] See Appendix I, "Forgiveness Meditation," by Jack Kornfield.

20. GENEROSITY

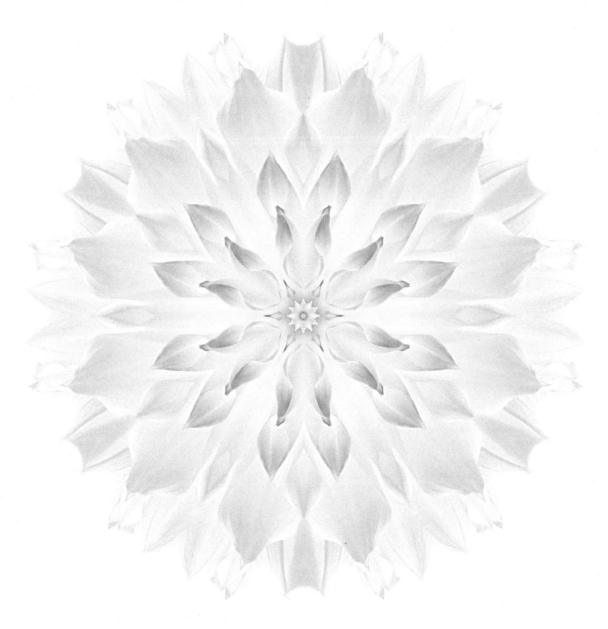

Spread your love everywhere you go.
- *Mother Teresa*

Giant White Dahlia

Generosity: Lighting the candle

A riddle: In Hell there is a great dining table. On it are bowls of the most aromatic stew you can imagine. Sitting across from each other, with the bowls between them, are two rows of people. Each person has a spoon with a handle so long that no matter how hard they try to stretch their arms, they can't manage to get even a single spoonful into their mouths. They cannot leave their seats and are in a state of perpetual, agonizing hunger. In Heaven, the setup is identical, but each member of this dining party is happy and well fed. What's the difference?

Answer: In Heaven, they are all feeding the person across from them.

Many of us who have been wounded as children withhold our generosity. We keep our love inside, as if there will be less for us if we give it away. As young children, we needed to receive more than we gave in order to survive. But, when we grow up getting less than we need, we may learn to hold onto what little we have as if our lives depended on it.

The strategies we unconsciously developed to protect ourselves from deprivation were necessary when we were younger. However, survival strategies often result in an impoverished life later on, a sense of always lacking and always wanting. Our wounds become our shields. To break free, we need to heal the woundedness that binds us.

The therapist/client relationship is not purely giving-based because it is also a professional relationship, but for me it has been good training for learning how to give without expecting anything back. Sometimes my own issues arise in reaction to difficult experiences in the therapy, but because I cannot act out my usual defensive patterns, I'm forced to come out from behind my shield and experience giving to my clients without reservation.

This process became clear to me early in my counseling training. While driving home after a late class, I reflected on a client I'd seen that morning, a young college student with a terrible family background who was alienated not only from his family but also from most of the people at his school. He was critical of every intervention I tried and quickly became proficient at spotting my vulnerabilities and exploiting them. Initially, I felt mainly my own defensiveness, and although I managed to contain it in the session, it sat with me all day.

I realized that if I remained self-protective, I could not help him. I knew that I couldn't work only with the easy, grateful clients; I had to help the jaded, angry, critical ones, too. But how? As I asked myself this question, the answer came: I had to love my clients the way I love children – generously and unconditionally.

In our next session, when the litany of complaints resumed, I asked him to pause. I said I understood how disappointing therapy had been so far and that I admired his courage for continuing to try. And I told him that although I might not be everything he hoped for in a therapist, I would do my best to help and I would stay with the process as long as he wanted me to.

The course of his treatment changed dramatically. I stopped frantically looking on the Internet between sessions to find ways to deal with his many symptoms, and I stopped dashing into my supervisor's office, desperate for advice. The therapy, I saw, would be as much about our relationship as it was about the issues he brought into the room. Of course, it always had been.

At the end of the school year, he took me up on my offer to stay with his process and became my first private client. I rented office space in Boston on Sundays and drove 40 miles each way from Gloucester just to see him.

By the time he completed therapy and was about to move out of the area, being in the room with him was a joy. He was a much more actualized version of himself, financially self-sufficient, participating in a wide variety of art-related activities, with many new friends. And, he had referred some of those friends to me, enabling me to more rapidly shift into full-time private practice. The generosity of heart I was able to find on that nocturnal ride home kindled a flame of generosity in him, and unbidden, he had returned my gift in spades.

During Chanukah, we use one candle to light all the other candles on the menorah. The illumination of that candle, the shamash, is undiminished by the process.

So it is with generosity.

21. GRACE

Grace is given not because we have done good works,
but in order that we may be able to do them.

   - *Saint Augustine of Hippo*

White Rose

GRACE: CONTINUATIONS

On February 21, 1993, at about 7:45pm, I was granted a form of grace that has shaped the rest of my life. On that evening I came within minutes of bleeding to death. Grace is tough, sometimes.

The initial warning sign was moderate gastrointestinal bleeding which, on the second day, brought me into the emergency room of St. Peter's Hospital in Albany, NY. The tentative diagnosis was lower bowel ulcers induced by a month on Motrin I'd taken for a shoulder injury. I allowed them to admit me only because the ER doctor warned that, although they couldn't run any tests till the following Monday, "Sometimes these things really let loose. You may not be able to get back here in time."

At first I was merely irritated by the inconvenience. It was a crisp Saturday afternoon, I had things to do, and I'd expected to have a few tests and go home. I became concerned only when the gastroenterologist they assigned to me said she didn't *think* they'd have to transfuse, but she was ordering blood of my type "just in case." She also said she didn't *think* they'd have to operate. Until that moment it hadn't occurred to me that they might transfuse, or operate, or that there was anything seriously wrong. Except for a little weakness, I felt fine.

I remained at St. Peter's all of Saturday and Sunday, drinking clear liquids and receiving IV fluids. By Sunday night, the bleeding stopped. The doctor ordered a colonoscopy prep. Her hope, and by then mine, was that they would find superficial ulcers, inject them with something to prevent further bleeding, and send me home in a couple of days with medications and a bland diet. I told her that I wanted to wait, that it seemed like a bad idea to stir up tissues that had only just stopped bleeding. But she insisted that short of exploratory surgery, this was the only way to find out what was wrong. Reluctantly, I consented.

An hour later, on my way back from my fourth trip to the bathroom, I blacked out before I could reach the nurse's call button. I remember weakly crying out "Help" and collapsing to my knees, fearing that my call would go unheard.

This fear was not groundless. A hospital is never quiet. Around the corner were two geriatric patients who moaned all day and late into the night. A nearby monitor's periodic beeps seemed to trigger their moans and cries, much as a siren might excite the neighborhood dogs. Even with ear plugs, I had been unable to screen them out.

"I'd rather be dead than end up like that," I said to my girlfriend earlier that day.

"You shouldn't say that!" she scolded. "God will hear!"

As I lost consciousness, I realized that my own call for help would sound no different from theirs, and I feared that, like the boy who cried wolf, nobody would distinguish the real emergency from the false alarm, perhaps not even God.

The next thing I remember is two nurses crouching beside me as I lay on my back in a pool of blood. I later learned they had found me only because my 83-year-old roommate, a stroke victim, had heard me fall and stumbled into the hallway for help. "David's on the floor!" he tried to say, but the nurses couldn't understand him. Luckily, his bed was by the window and when they guided him back there, they had to pass me on the way.

When they roused me, my blood pressure was 70/30, and I felt very cold. The nurses put a sheet under me, got a couple of nurse's aides from the hallway, and with their help hoisted me onto the bed, where they inserted a second IV. At first they thought they could stabilize me with fluids, and I did feel a little stronger, but as my blood pressure began to rise, more blood poured out, bathing me in its sudden warmth.

The gastroenterologist arrived and started a

transfusion, and that, too, seemed to help at first, but again, as my blood pressure rose, the rate of bleeding increased, this time pumping blood out faster than they could push it back in. They kept saying, "You're not going to die, don't worry, you're not going to die." "I'm cold," I kept telling them, reminding myself of the Snowden character in Joseph Heller's *Catch 22*.

They attempted to start another unit of blood, but they couldn't find an entry point – my pressure was so low that the veins in my arms had collapsed. Then they stopped telling me I was going to be all right and started calling for things *stat*.

Until that moment, I had been curiously detached from my situation, as if I were at home watching TV and all this fuss was happening to someone else. But when I saw that the doctor and nurses no longer seemed to be in control, it became clear to me that I might have only a couple of minutes to live.

I was completely unafraid. As the room began to fade out, I stopped paying attention to the frantic medical staff surrounding me. Instead, my focus shifted onto an interior landscape. In my mind's eye, I saw a series of line graphs, one laid on top of another like the maps of the human body's systems in anatomy textbooks. Each graph represented how close I had come to following my path. The top one tracked my vocation; it dipped down in the bad times – the longest being my recent decade as a technical writer – and up again after I quit the corporate world and returned to graduate school. Lower charts showed similar patterns in other aspects of my life: family, romantic relationships, spirituality, creativity, others I no longer recall. There was a break in each of the charts at what I took to be the present moment, and then suddenly all the lines extended sharply upward, into my uncertain future.

As I lost all bodily sensation, I felt a surge of regret not so much for the things I had done as for what I might never get the chance to do. The graphs vanished.

In their place, hanging in the darkness, the Scales of Justice appeared, on which were equally balanced the pluses and minuses of my life. This image also passed, and with it my regret. I felt ready to face, with equanimity, whatever was to come.

Yet I didn't want to die. So with my last conscious thought, I made a request: "If there is a God, and you're listening, I think I know what to do with my life now, and I'd like a chance to complete it." Then the room and my body faded out and "I" went into another space entirely.

I was in a black, amorphous cave whose surfaces glinted like moonlight on choppy seas. In the distance was a vague, greenish pool of light. I had no sense of a body or of ever having had one, or of my own identity, or even of being a human being. I was simply awareness. I felt no anxiety, heard no sounds, had no memories, thought no thoughts. I was more alone than I'd ever been, but it didn't bother me at all. I was unaware of the passage of time and felt a calmness more pervasive than any I have experienced, before or since.

Then my consciousness leaped forward and I saw that the illumination came from a figure seated at a small, square table made of fuzzy tubes of yellow-green light. From my vantage point, this figure, also made of the same tubes of fuzzy light, looked like a child's sketch of a man, with a circle for a head, an oval for a body, and stick-like arms and legs. He seemed to be leaning on the table with his left elbow, chin in his left hand, while his right hand rested on the tabletop, holding what may have been a pen, as if he were poised in thought.

My sense was that this creature was me, the me I was born with, the me I would die with, my essential Self; that it was waiting; and that it could wait indefinitely. I did not wonder what would happen next. I, too, was content to wait, being him and watching him at the same time.

My consciousness zoomed forward again, and as it did, the figure at the table turned his head toward me. I could see the outline of his face, the sharp angle of his chin. His nose seemed pointed and elongated and his mouth was frozen in a half smile that felt oddly chilling.

A moment later I was back in my hospital bed, someone else's blood flowing into both arms from three IV needles. A nurse was reading off my blood pressure: "70/30. 80/50. 90/60...." The doctor's narrow face loomed over me, a nervous smile. "There, that's better," she said, flushed and sweaty. "Isn't that better?"

The last 20-plus years of recovery, reintegration, and reorientation have been a good news, bad news affair. The bad news is that coming back was far more difficult than I could have imagined that cold night in 1993. The good news is that it has also been a gift, a form of grace that has extended far beyond getting what I think of as "extra time."

First the bad news.

There were many physical changes. Early that Monday morning, I bled again, briefly, and surgery was performed that my medical malpractice attorneys would later prove was drastic and unnecessary. After surgery, I experienced pain I didn't know a person could feel without losing consciousness. Subsequently, I have required many medical treatments and two additional surgeries to partially correct the damages done. From the bleeding incident itself, my vision and my hearing were damaged, and the way my mind works has been subtly altered. Left-brain functions such as math, logic, and spelling became more difficult, though right-brain functions seem to have compensated, over time.

Then there were the life changes. The St. Peter's Hospital incident devastated my finances, destroyed a relationship that likely would have led to marriage and a family, and derailed my English PhD. Initially uplifting, the near-death experience itself produced a sense of profound disorientation. For a decade, I felt as if I were floating between two worlds, not quite who I had been, not yet who I was becoming. I had returned to a child-like innocence that allowed dangerous people to enter my life. The experience also fostered the naïve belief that, because I had beaten death, none of the rules I'd lived by necessarily applied, and I made decisions that, in retrospect, were incredibly reckless and had substantial negative impact, though they made complete sense to me at the time.

The good news is a shorter but more potent list.

This second time around, I have been able, finally, to forgive my parents and to overcome the limitations my childhood defenses and resentments had propagated. Creativity and intuition blossomed, and I became an artist and then a therapist, activities that have given me a purposeful way to live. Though I am in no hurry to get there, I am no longer afraid of death.

And then there is the question, Why am I still here? Given the amount of blood I lost and the rapidity with which I lost it, I should have died. The bleeding stopped only because my blood pressure was so low – 50/0, "the blood pressure of a corpse," as the chief resident involved in my case later put it – that clotting finally occurred. Answering this question has been the impetus for most of the positive changes I have made. I've often returned to the vision I had just before entering the near-death space and have tried to keep the lines of the graphs moving in an upward direction. It has been crucially important to complete the life I then imagined.

Now, I am startled, daily, by grace: by the miraculousness of everything that is, all of which seems as improbable as my own second coming. I no longer take anything for granted. I seem, still, to be evolving, refining, and recombining. I don't know what the future will bring.

But then, nobody else does, either.

22. GRATITUDE

Gratitude is the fairest blossom which springs from the
soul.

 - *Henry Ward Beecher*

White and Yellow Daffodil

GRATITUDE: LISTS

During my recuperation from a brush with death, a high school friend sent me a letter. In it, he hypothesized that as a survivor of near-death, every moment for me must be exquisitely sweet, a precious gift, in ways he could not imagine. At first, he was mostly right. Despite the pain, my initial response *was* celebratory. But the celebration was relatively short-lived and bittersweet. As weeks became months and months became years, the glow gradually diminished. Yielding to the numerous problems the experience of almost dying had also initiated, gratitude faded and a more troubled self re-emerged. Returning to that place of celebration has been a process.

Grateful people are generally more satisfied with their lives and relationships, cope better with difficulties, and are more generous, empathetic, and self-accepting. But despite these many benefits, many of us have a hard time feeling gratitude.

Often, early deprivation gets in the way. When there isn't enough of what we need – money, warmth, praise, joy, many other things – we intuitively respond by feeling deprived. We may carry this deprivation forward into adulthood and see life mainly as a struggle to get what we need. We often became good at making do, learning to be independent, acting assertively. But we don't learn to fully experience what is already there for us, if only we were open to taking it in. And so we grow cynical and jaded, mistaking an internal barrier for an external lack.

Or, deprivation may leave us hungry for more. If we're grateful for what we *have*, we may ask ourselves, what will motivate us to get *more*? But always wanting more does not make us happy. It just makes us always wanting.

An alternative approach is to start from a place of gratitude. Then we say, "I am happy with what I have now. If I get more, I will be happy then, too."

The difference between these two approaches came to me most clearly at a Buddhist retreat held at a local college. I requested a half-hour meeting with one of the monks there. We sat together on a hillside overlooking the dining hall and ate our lunches while I talked with him about feelings of hurt, betrayal, and despair that followed the difficult ending of a long relationship.

"I understand your feelings," he said, "but this way of looking at love is too limited. You think it comes only from these people, and now it is gone. But love comes from many places." He held out his sandwich. "The baker who made this bread shows us love. Yes, it is his business, but the bread is very good and there is love in it. And there are the trees and the grass. They give us oxygen – without them we could not live." He looked up at the sky. "And the sun gives us warmth."

As he continued to point out human and non-human sources of love, I felt a shift inside. Until that moment, the idea that "the universe loves us" had seemed so abstract it was meaningless. But now, listening to this young monk as he took in the love of the cosmos, I vicariously experienced his gratitude, and I carry these feelings with me to this day.

A simple but effective tool for counteracting our in-built tendency to focus on shortages is the gratitude list. It is a way to reinforce the feeling that regardless of what we lack, we also have many things for which to be grateful. We may not have all the wealth we want, the health we want, the relationships we want, the things we want, but when we list what we *do* have, we have a lot.

Most of my own gratitude lists I keep in my head, but from time to time I write them down. I started one for this essay. I soon realized I could spend hours naming things for which I feel grateful, and that the list of what I'm unhappy about, even in the worst of times, is always much shorter. Here, in the order in which they occurred to me, are the first 50:

Being alive. Being human. Coming of age in 1969. All five of my senses. Intuition. My friends and family. Women I've loved. Beauty. Sadness. Joy. Wonder. Curiosity. Imagination. All the arts. All the sciences. Other animals. Plants. Rocks. Clouds. The blue sky. The ocean. Mountains. Children. Gadgets. Cars and motorcycles. Things to figure out. People who figure things out. Intelligence. Hope. Coffee. Chocolate-covered almonds. Memories. Greek yogurt. Strawberries. Apples. Books. Meditation. Movies. Music. Air. Water. Land. Humor. Babies. Flowers. Silence. Wind. Lightning. Compassion. Popsicles.

What's on your gratitude list today?

23. HEALING

Healing is a matter of time, but it is sometimes also a
matter of opportunity.

 - *Hippocrates*

Peony 'Bowl of Beauty'

Healing: Inner child, wounded healer

Contrary to popular wisdom, timing is not everything and time alone cannot heal all wounds. What heals wounds is care, and what heals the deepest wounds is persistent, trusted caring. That caring can come from many sources, among them friends, family, and professionals, as well as, with practice, from our own internal, wounded healers.

Friends and, sometimes, family have carried me through the majority of life's hardships. Support groups and group therapy have also been pivotal, particularly while recovering from PTSD after my brush with death. Creative work, too, has always been important to emotional healing. But reaching the deepest, innermost hurts has required developing what Carl Jung called a "wounded healer" and connecting it directly to my inner child.

I began inner child work in my early 30s. As my therapist and I worked through the problems I had originally come to her for, our attention gradually shifted to older issues. Like many trauma sufferers, I had blocked out large segments of my past. Therapy became like an archaeological dig, both of us sifting through the sands of time together, seeking artifacts from my personal history that would account for my current symptoms and patterns.

In one guided visualization, I encountered an image of a sealed, bomb-like container at my core, with a six-inch-thick titanium shell. At first I believed this shell contained nuclear rage, as anger was the first strong feeling I remembered. But as we continued our exploration, the shell gradually became first translucent and then transparent. I could see that what it held was not a bomb but a frightened little boy. Later, in a dream, I envisioned a landscape dotted with similar translucent capsules half-buried in a field. I understood them to be parts of myself that I had concealed there long before. My years of work in therapy had blown away the covering soil, and these time capsules, glowing in the twilight, awaited reopening.

Many of us have, inside, a child who has been injured, and we also have, often unrecognized, a healer. Because our internal healers contain the wounded child, they have the capacity to respond to the needs of that little boy or girl better than anyone else on the planet. Instead of being disabled by their woundedness, these healers can tune in to the pain of the child with understanding and compassion. This inner child / wounded healer relationship allows us to experience the most complete healing.

Since my first round of therapy, I have used several strategies to become more intimate with my inner child and to become more cognizant of my wounded healer.

The inner child / wounded healer relationship started, for me, with another visualization. In it, I imagined walking by the ocean and seeing, coming toward me, a little boy. As he drew nearer, I saw that he was a six-year-old version of me. He seemed lost, but when I asked him where he belonged, he turned his head away and stared at the ground. Unsure what to do next, but wanting to help, I picked up an interesting rock and offered it to him. Hesitantly, he accepted it.

Later, I incorporated this visualization into a technique that uses writing with both hands to create a dialogue between my inner child and wounded healer. I'd close my eyes and imagine meeting the little boy on the now-familiar path. Then I'd open my eyes and write, on a piece of paper, "Are you okay?" with my dominant hand. Switching the pen to my non-dominant hand, I'd write a response as if I were that little boy. Writing with the non-dominant hand forced me to slow my verbal expression to the speed of a child. Going back and forth between dominant and non-dominant hands, being first the wounded healer and then the inner child, I came to understand what was hurting and how to help.

In my early inner child work, I focused mainly on connecting with younger and younger versions of my little boy. The littlest of the little boys was three. As I have continued to explore the inner child / wounded healer relationship, I've also encountered a troubled adolescent, an angry teenager, a fiery college student, a twenty-something young man adrift, and numerous other incarnations of my younger selves. They are like Russian nesting dolls, at their core a very young, uninjured child who holds my greatest joy.

When I work with clients and their inner children, I use many of the same techniques I have found helpful in developing my personal inner child / wounded healer relationship. Through similar processes, clients learn to move through the layers, opening their own time capsules, returning to themselves the precious parts they have preserved, adding to their wholeness.

24. HOPE

"Hope" is the thing with feathers –
That perches in the soul –
And sings the tune without the words –
And never stops – at all –
  - *Emily Dickinson*

White and Orange Daffodil

Hope: The thing with feathers

Shortly before I was to meet my first therapy client, my supervisor advised that if I accomplished nothing more in a first session, I should at least instill hope. "If they don't have hope," he said, "they won't come back, and you can't help them."

Hope is not a panacea, but it is a balm. Without hope, we are buffeted by our difficulties and can, sometimes irrevocably, lose our way. In its presence, almost anything is endurable.

The ancient Greeks conveyed the palliative power of hope in the Pandora story. Pandora was the first mortal woman. She came to Earth with a box she was told never to open. But she also received the gift of curiosity. When she could no longer resist temptation, she took a peek inside the box and thereby let loose all the evils of mankind. Pandora quickly shut the box, but by then only one item remained inside: hope. Before she'd opened the box, Earth had been an innocent, untroubled place, with no need for hope. But once evils were released into the world, life became unsustainable without it. In an act of repentance for what she had done, Pandora opened the box a second time and released hope.

I frequently remember my first supervisor's comment about hope, the kind that urges us on when we feel we can't continue. How do we instill *that* hope in the hopeless, or in ourselves when we have lost it?

Although it has been a long time since I heard that advice, hope is still the foundation of my work. These are some of the strategies I typically use (in approximately this order) not only to instill hope, but also to allow it to grow and encourage progress in clients' lives. These are not specialized therapist techniques. Anyone can do them.

1. Validate. "Yes, I understand why you feel like that." Before we can accept help from anyone, we need to feel understood and accepted by them. Although it may seem counterintuitive, validating feelings of hopelessness and despair lets people know that even in their darkest moments, you accept them, opening a door to connection and trust.

2. Normalize. "Anyone might feel this way in your situation." When we feel hopeless, assurance that our despair is not crazy helps to ground us. From a more grounded state, we can begin to move out of hopelessness.

3. Accompany. "We can sort that out together." Demonstrating willingness to accompany the hopeless in their difficulties can generate a little light. To accompany someone who is without hope, all we need is empathy and the ability to remain grounded ourselves, sensing their pain but not being swept away by it. Reminding the hopeless that we, too, have had dark nights of the soul and have recovered from them inspires confidence that they can do it, too.

4. Mirror. "I see how terrible you feel, but even so, I can sense your strength and courage." Those who can't see their own light need others to see it for them and to gently reflect it back, so that they can eventually embrace it.

5. Notice. "You did *that*? Great!" When we are hopeless, we need others to point out positive changes we might otherwise overlook. Taking the smallest action pushes against the paralysis of hopelessness, igniting a tiny flame that can, eventually, grow into a bonfire of hopefulness.

6. Reinforce. "Wow, that's a *lot* more than you were able to do last week!" Hope can't take root without monitoring, encouraging, and validating progress. Small "experiments" help to challenge the limits that hopelessness imposes.

7. Scale. "On a scale of 1 to 10, where '1' is how you felt when things were as bad as they ever were, and '10' is how they'll be when you're really happy with your life, what's your score these days?" Scaling is a tool to counter-act inertia. Not only does it provides a means for people to evaluate their progress, it also implies that progress is possible. Periodically reapplying the scaling process helps to distinguish what works from what impedes progress.

8. Advise. Last and often least helpful is advice. Offered too early in the process, advice is usually rejected because hopeless people don't believe they can follow it, or that even if they could, they doubt it would do any good. Save advice for later, and then give it only if the person in recovery from hopelessness wants it. In its early stages, hope, the "thing with feathers" in Emily Dickinson's poem, can be a fragile thing. Treat it with great care.

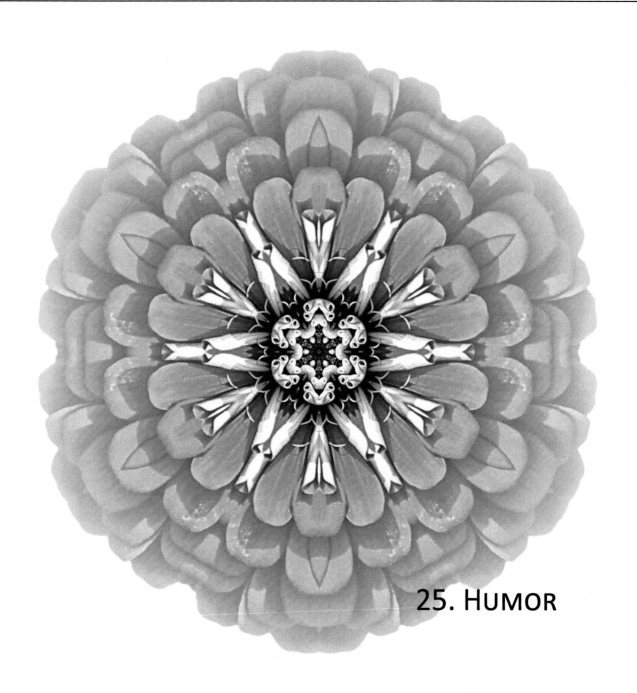

25. HUMOR

When humor goes, there goes civilization.
 - *Erma Bombeck*

Violet Zinnia Elegans

HUMOR: THE LANGUAGE OF LAUGHTER

Long ago, when I worked as a technical writer in New Hampshire, I carpooled from Cambridge with my editor. In one of our many animated conversations, we were talking about the possibility of nuclear war and I cracked a joke. He turned to me and said, gravely, "You can't joke about nuclear war." I thought for a moment, then responded, "What else can I do about it?"

When I was a boy, *Reader's Digest* had a humor column called "Laughter, the Best Medicine," and it turns out they got that right. Laughter relaxes muscles, decreases stress hormones, boosts the immune system, releases endorphins, improves blood flow, eases anxiety, helps diffuse conflict, and increases connection between people. Norman Cousins, former *Saturday Review* editor-in-chief, claimed that watching old Marx Brothers comedies helped cure him of a potentially fatal spinal disorder. "Laugh and the world laughs with you, cry and you cry alone" seems, also, to have more than a grain of truth. A recent *British Medical Journal* study established that a good mood is contagious out to at least three degrees of separation.

Like Gloucester poet Charles Olson, "I have had to learn the simplest things last," and one of them was humor. As a college student, I noticed that the ironic comments that passed for wit among my high school friends didn't travel well. I set out to discover what else made people laugh.

I started with one joke, learning by trial and error how best to tell it. Next I strung several jokes together into a routine. I experimented with short jokes, long jokes, stupid jokes, groaners. A personal triumph was inventing my own shaggy dog story, based on a repetitive series of threatening letters I'd received from the subscription department of *New Times* magazine.[1] With joke-telling somewhat under my belt, I went on to play with punning, double entendres, repetition, timing, and incongruity. I tried physical humor, ranging from making bizarre faces to head-slapping and other silly gestures. I learned to imitate foreign accents and to invent personae to speak in them.

As my repertoire expanded, I became more attuned to audience. Children giggled when I inserted made-up words in the middle of sentences. Making up words with girlfriends gave us a more intimate, private language. When I worked in construction, inserting expletives inside other words ("Unbef**kinglievable!") helped make me one of the guys. In Italy, I discovered that putting the wrong ending on a word made Italians of almost any age laugh. Sometimes, the quest for what tickled someone's funny bone was daunting. Finding out how to make one girlfriend laugh took five years! (She was partial to pratfalls and penis jokes.) My informal study of humor didn't make me a comedian, but it did help me see that there is a language of humor, and each of us has our own dialect.

In my professional life, humor is ever-present. I watch for hints of it and send out gentle forays whenever humor might help to lighten a load, break up a quarrel, or provide broader perspective. Even in the midst of discussing frustration, anger, betrayal, and grief, client sessions are sprinkled with irony, wit, and wordplay.

Sharing someone's language of humor can be pivotal to forging a therapeutic alliance. I once worked with a young man who had a long history of unwillingness to participate in therapy. Nobody "got" him, he said. He had, however, a keenly derisive sense of humor, and I went with it. He insulted my "big Jewish nose," mocked me for "decrepitude," and tested my patience with relentless punning. Gradually, his hostility evolved into a private language of humor between us, and that opened a pathway to his sharing his difficulties – and his triumphs.

I encourage clients to use humor to cope with trying situations. This is especially helpful with children. One young client hated writing assignments because his teacher expected him to be compliant and "like school." To redirect the helpless rage he experienced, we experimented with irony and sarcasm. He was thrilled to discover that his teacher had no clue about what he was really saying. Another boy used humor to repel bullies. When they taunted him, he either responded with non sequiturs or acted as if what they were saying made his day. They thought he was crazy and twirled their fingers around their ears, but they soon left him alone.

"Were it not for my little jokes," Abraham Lincoln once commented, "I could not bear the burdens of this office." Perhaps we can learn by example from the man who shepherded us through our most horrific period and, even when our circumstances seem most dire, see in them, as he did, the fundamental humor of our human condition.

---

[1] See Appendix II, "New Times and Shaggy Dogs."

26. ILLUMINATION

Enlightenment consists not merely in the seeing of
luminous shapes and visions, but in making the darkness
visible.

  - *Carl Jung*

Red and Yellow Dahlia

ILLUMINATION: INTERWEAVINGS

il·lu·mi·na·tion (noun)

1. a. The act of illuminating.
   b. The state of being illuminated.
2. A source of light.
3. Spiritual or intellectual enlightenment.
4. Clarification; elucidation.
5. a. The art or act of decorating a text, page, or initial letter with ornamental designs, miniatures, or lettering.
   b. An example of this art.
6. Physics: The luminous flux per unit area at any point on a surface exposed to incident light.

Beginning with a dictionary definition may be a throwback to fifth grade, but here it seems right. It was in fifth grade, at age 10, that the interweaving strands of my personal illumination began.

10

I took my first pictures with my family's twin-lens Brownie camera when I was about 10. It's difficult, now, to remember what I photographed, and none of my pictures from that era remain, but I still recall the thrill of the scene in front of me illuminating the tiny viewfinder's ground-glass screen and then, some days later, reappearing as a booklet of square, deckle-edged, black-and-white prints – frozen moments preserved, I imagined, for all time. At that age, I also ventured, tentatively, into spirituality via Hebrew school and science fiction and began to think about time, consciousness, the boundaries and origin of the universe, and mortality.

My first experience of time as a continuum occurred when I was riding my red Schwinn bicycle past a neighbor's house. I stopped abruptly, and as I gazed at the simple brick facade, the white trim, the unkempt bushes, I thought, "This is just one second in my life, and I'll never remember it again." But that moment is one of my most vivid childhood memories. Perhaps I remember it because that was the year both of my grandfathers died. Or maybe it was the Hebrew school readings from the

Book of Genesis, or the science fiction stories. Or perhaps 10 is just when most boys begin to understand time and death. In any case, from that point on, time had a kind of linearity and my own life an end point.

By high school I'd graduated from box cameras to twin-lens reflex cameras, SLRs with interchangeable lenses, and a Robot Star – a spring-wound camera used by Luftwaffe pilots to record kills.

I discovered I had a knack for composition and for capturing expressions. I photographed friends, family members, street scenes, and nature, and even found occasional paid work taking pictures of babies, children, and aspiring actresses and models. Seeing people through the eye of the camera was both a shield and a way to connect. I learned to process and print black-and-white and color film, and the darkroom soon became an integral part of what photography meant to me.

20

In college, I began to let go of Judaism and grew increasingly attracted to Eastern religions and practices. In the summer following my sophomore year in college, I hitchhiked across the United States, learned Transcendental Meditation in Berkeley and traveled back home through Canada, arriving with a quarter in my pocket and an expanded outlook. I began to read seriously in Hinduism, Buddhism, Sufism, and the works of the Armenian-Russian mystic G. I. Gurdjieff, as well as seminal writings of psychologists from Sigmund Freud to Fritz Perls. I spent a semester volunteering in a state mental hospital and also briefly entered therapy, where I first delved into a childhood I had unwittingly pushed aside by forgetting everything that had happened to me before age 10.

My personal illumination continued during six years in New York City in the mid '70s. I revisited therapy with a pastoral counselor, reread the Bible while writing a story about a man who thought he was God, and read widely in the mythology, art history, and folktales of China, Japan, India, and Egypt.

I soon began to combine photography and writing. I carried with me a tape recorder, a notepad, and two or three cameras in a homemade camera bag. I photographed the bums, bag ladies, vendors, muggers, pimps, prostitutes and others who, like me, roamed the streets and subways of Manhattan and Brooklyn. A self-styled anthropologist, I blended into a world largely ignored by native New Yorkers but shockingly vivid to me. I'd walk down the street constantly framing images in my mind, mentally shooting hundreds of pictures in a single trip downtown from the fifth-floor walk-up on West 98th St. and Broadway I shared with two Israelis. Forty years before Google Glass, I longed to have a camera embedded in my forehead, a third eye. (The Robot Star was the next best thing.) I wrote a book that combined the images I was shooting with stories about street people I interviewed, a kind of illuminated manuscript inspired by the collaboration of James Agee and Walker Evans in their book *Let Us Now Praise Famous Men*.

Although I left engineering school after my first year of college, I never lost interest in technology as a way of apprehending the world. From the start, I experimented with ways to push the boundaries of the photographic medium. Much of my shooting was nocturnal, and when the level of literal illumination was insufficient to fully render a scene, I enhanced the negatives with special developers and chromium intensifiers that brought out more detail but also accentuated the harshness of the lives I was recording. As each picture emerged in the developer tray, I felt again the fascination I'd had as a child with my Brownie camera and deckled prints.

30

My 20s were exciting times, perhaps the most exciting of my life. But I was like Icarus flying too close to the sun, and by age 30 my wax wings melted.

In 1979, I left New York City, drifted around Europe for a couple of months, lived in artist colonies, and finally landed in a small apartment in Cambridge, MA, as a graduate student in creative writing at Boston University. But the master's degree in writing I'd hoped would usher me into a teaching career was not enough to get me a full-time college job. I had injured my back the previous

summer and could no longer support myself doing construction, the work that for years had supported my writing and photography habit. In what felt like an act of desperation, I took a crash course in computer science and soon found a job as a technical writer.

Creative writing had flared briefly and brightly while I was in the program at B.U., but once I started to write about computers, the flame went out, and I descended into the darkness of depression. Without a darkroom, I lost interest in creating photographs, and along with writing and photography, conscious spiritual pursuit also dimmed.

Robert Bly, in his landmark book about men, *Iron John*, talks about how in many indigenous cultures, the young men are required to live for a time in the ash piles surrounding their villages. Time in the ashes, he says, is time for the death of the ego-bound boy; it prepares him to be more resilient and accepting when difficulty shows up in later life. My 10 years as a technical writer was my time in the ashes. But it was not without its redeeming qualities. In its darkness, I sought relief through psychotherapy and began my first serious round of digging into my shadow side. With my therapist's guidance, I explored both the tragedies and the treasures buried deep in my subconscious, and a necessary consolidation occurred. The pinpoint light of therapy helped me not only to change my awareness but also my actions. It initiated deeper transformations that eventually led me out of that darkness and paved the way for a more nuanced response to what was yet to come.

40

My 40s were marked by my almost literal death and rebirth and a consequent re-illumination of creativity and spirituality.

Shortly after my 40th birthday, I quit tech writing and moved to Albany, NY, to attend a PhD program in English and, I hoped, to complete a novel that would serve as my dissertation. The near-death experience I had the following year, despite its many complexities, accelerated the resurrection of my creative and spiritual sides by enabling me to directly experience an inner light in myself and others. (See the essay "Grace.") At the time, I thought it had saved me the effort of 20 years of study and meditation. Although I now see that a window is all it really was, it is windows that the light shines through.

In the hands of a gifted psychotherapist who was practiced in most of the major spiritual traditions, therapy also went to a deeper level. With his help, I was able to put the pieces of my fragmented self back together, and to learn how to keep the inner light going. So far, nothing since then has been able to completely extinguish it.

50

At 50, photography returned. I bought a digital camera and found myself drawn to patterns of color and light, rather than the harsh street scenes I had photographed in New York City. Because of my long experience with computers, digital technology came to me easily and it opened previously unimaginable photographic possibilities. I eagerly tinkered with images, at first merely trying to improve color and contrast. I soon realized that because they were computer files, I could also do much more. I strived to create forms that felt beautiful and meaningful. Phototransformations such as the Flower Mandalas emerged as I transitioned from documentary photography into art, integrating both the left-brain and right-brain sides of my nature.

This decade also launched a deeper dive into psychological and spiritual illumination.

In group therapy, I worked through the remaining trauma of my Albany experience. As I was leaving the group, the leader, a Buddhist, suggested I attend a five-day retreat where Thich Nhat Hanh and 50 of his monks and nuns were to lead some 850 retreatants. There were two slots left and I took one. A decade later, I am still practicing what I learned there.

That retreat, which I came to think of as "Buddhist boot camp," occurred during the summer before I began a therapy internship at Massachusetts College of Art.

Changes in my personality and focus – consequences of the near-death experience and its related trauma – had drawn me back to a desire to pursue psychotherapy as a career that was present even in my first year of college. (And perhaps long before then. Most therapists start out as child psychologists, early on becoming highly attuned to the difficult emotions surrounding us as children.) Rather than completing my English PhD, I entered a master's program in counseling psychology. I threw myself into therapist training, attending institutes and workshops to supplement what I was learning in my program. Late out of the gate, I wanted to hit the ground running.

The summer of the Thich Nhat Hanh retreat, I also made my first Flower Mandala, the Dandelion Head image that accompanies the first essay in this book. Indirectly, mandala-making, an integrating process that focuses on the inner self, further inclined me to becoming a therapist. As I have developed my practice as a healer, creating mandalas continues to help me stay balanced. The mandalas have become a means for processing the suffering I feel from my clients, reminiscent of the Buddhist *tonglen* practice. In *tonglen*, on the in-breath, practitioners visualize taking in the suffering of others. As they hold the breath, they imagine transforming it. Then, on the out-breath, they give back loving kindness. Similarly, I use mandala-making to convert suffering into beauty and, by displaying the resultant images, offer the product of this transformation to others.

60

My 60s appear to be a decade of integration, a time of weaving together the multiple strands of illumination that have lighted my path. This book is one outcome of that integrating process. It brings together the apparently disparate methods I have used to apprehend reality – technology, photography, writing, spirituality, and psychotherapy – into one place, where I can see them as the singular form they have always been.

It will be interesting to see what happens next.

27. INDEPENDENCE

No man is an island,
Entire of itself.
  - *John Donne*

Pink Hibiscus

Independence: Declarations

As an American, I have valued independence most of my life. Independence is highly prized in this country. We associate it with positive qualities such as self-sufficiency, self-reliance, self-determination, autonomy, and – most of all – with freedom. We see independence as our greatest national strength and promote it, sometimes aggressively, as a global ideal. But what is independence, really?

For some it begins with defiance. My own independence started that way. As a first-year engineering student in 1969, I proudly wore a button with a Greek Ω (the electrical symbol for resistance) on my faded denim jacket. My peers and I rebelled against anyone and anything we deemed oppressive, graduating from high school protests against dress codes and the administration's invasions of privacy to massive demonstrations against racism and the War in Vietnam. Now, although I still believe in the issues we fought for, I wonder if we were truly independent then. Defiance is shaped by the same parameters as what we defy. In the name of equality, we set up a new dichotomy: "They" were the hard hats, the Establishment, the Military-Industrial Complex, the status quo, while "we" were the students, the hippies, the Left, the Revolution. Only much later did my generation begin the difficult task of true self-examination.

Others see independence as avoiding entanglements. The roots of this view usually extend far into the past. As infants and toddlers, we develop an avoidant attachment style when our caregivers don't appropriately respond to our dependent needs; instead, they discourage crying or asking for help, and they emphasize autonomy. So we learn to meet our own needs instead. We grow up to become adults who see ourselves as self-sufficient and not requiring help or close relationships, believing that deep connections will weaken us and cost us our autonomy. But avoidant independence is not true independence, either.

As children, we develop a secure attachment style when our caregivers respond to us promptly, appropriately, and consistently. We learn we can count on them, and so we're free to explore our environments and connect with others, knowing we will have a safe place to return to. We grow up to become securely attached adults, comfortable with both intimacy and autonomy, where each person in a relationship feels whole, free to connect without fusing, and able to separate without distancing or anxiety.

I became aware of the adult ramifications of secure and avoidant childhood attachment styles during my first technical writing job. In my early weeks at Digital Equipment Corporation, I worked frantically, responding to constant deadline pressure by literally running from one work station to another to keep up with what felt like an impossible schedule. After a while, I noticed that a co-worker in the cubicle adjoining mine seemed, somehow, to have plenty of time. At first I assumed that she was just walking through her job, but her work was as accurate and complete as mine. Eventually, I asked her how she managed. "I go to the developers when I need help," she said. Until that moment, I was unaware that asking for help was an option, or that it was as valuable a skill as self-reliance.

Disempowered forms of independence may protect us from the pain of being dominated or neglected, but they ultimately limit our real freedom. For most of us, the best fit for our inborn natures is not defiant independence or avoidant independence, but the balance of independence and connection of the securely attached child – to be complete in ourselves, but also to become, in our personal relationships and in the larger community, *interdependent*.

Real independence recognizes our fundamental interdependence. To achieve it, we must challenge the self-protective patterns we developed in our earlier lives, owning who we truly are, breaking the chains of disempowered independence so something new can occur. Realizing my own interdependence is still a work in progress, but each step in this direction is deeply fulfilling. Letting go of defiance has permitted me to more fully explore my innate nature. Learning to ask for help has broadened and deepened my connections without compromising my autonomy.

Centuries ago, English poet John Donne wrote, "No man is an island, entire of itself. Each is a piece of the continent, a part of the main." As our current struggle with global climate change demonstrates, we are all interdependently connected to the whole: person to person, nation to nation, creature to creature, to every living and non-living thing. By embracing interdependence on this scale, we are better able to implement lasting change not only in ourselves, but in our world.

28. JOY

Joy is not in things; it is in us.
  - *Richard Wagner*

Pink Peony

JOY: OPENINGS

What draws many of us to babies is their near-constant sense of excitement and wonder. This is our natural state, to feel joy about being alive and in the world. Unfortunately, life experiences and our responses to them can cover that joy with layers of difficulty, burying it so deep it can seem as if it never existed. Then, we may seek "happiness" from external sources – in people, experiences, things – forgetting that what we are hoping to find is already inside us. This pattern is not unique to our complex times. As William Wordsworth observed two centuries ago, "The world is too much with us; late and soon, getting and spending, we lay waste our powers…. We have given our hearts away."

Trauma and the deeply ingrained pessimism that often springs from it can mask joy. So can pain, depression, anxiety, fear, loneliness, isolation, sadness, anger, jealousy, hatred, and betrayal. But it's still there, trying to break out, like a dandelion pushing through a crack in the pavement.

In the weeks following my brush with death in Albany, my body was mangled and my mind felt as if a bomb had exploded in the middle of my head. But I was determined, at least, to regain my mobility. Although it was winter and I lived in a rural area, twice each day I forced myself outside with a makeshift cane in my hand and a coat over my pajamas and robe. I walked. At first I got only 20 or 30 feet before I had to turn back, but with each successive foray, I extended my range. After a few weeks, I made it all the way to the highway, about half a mile.

As I sat on a rock, resting until I had the strength to make the return trip, I looked out at the snow-covered fields, the yellow construction vehicles in a nearby subdivision, the rushing cars and trucks obediently whisking their occupants to wherever they were going. I felt the cold air on my hands, the numbness of my toes, and watched the fog of my breath. And I felt a surge of invigoration and the sensation of things suddenly clicking.

I thought, "I'm back."

What had returned was access to the intrinsic joy from which I'd been separated much of my life, the layers covering it stripped away by the rebirthing process of the near-death experience. Later difficulties distanced me from joy again, but the effect of that plugged-in moment was profound. Now, even in the darkest times, I'm still aware of a tiny, joyful bud wanting to poke through the concrete, and sometimes that awareness alone is enough to enable it to blossom.

The trick to joy is not in acquiring, because there is no end to acquiring, nor in ending pain and suffering, because pain and suffering cannot always be ended, and even when they are, they will inevitably recur. The trick is instead to find joy even in the midst of lacking, even in the midst of pain and suffering. It's there, all the time, if we open our hearts to experiencing it.

Each of us has our particular ways to access joy. Some find it in music, singing, dancing, laughing, a sunset, a snowfall, a flower. Motorcycling brings me joy, as does talking with friends, connecting intimately, the moment in a movie theater when the lights go down, a flash of insight, listening to the ocean, playing with children – and even a simple breath, when I remind myself that at one point it was uncertain I would take another, and that at some other point it is certain I will not. Any of these things, and many more, can allow the joy that's always already there to emerge.

"What brings you joy?" I recently asked a young friend. "Everything!" he said. Even pain and sadness, he explained, bring out joy, because previously he would have fled from them. Now, for him, the most difficult emotions can still feel joyful, because he knows he is no longer numb.

I live in an area where sodium streetlights were recently installed. At night, to keep out the bright yellow glare, I hung light-blocking shades. When I raise the shades in the morning, sunlight filters through the Venetian blinds. When I open the blinds, it comes into the room in a rush.

Joy is like that. It is rolling up the shades, opening the blinds, letting the light in and then basking in its warmth and brilliance, like a cat in a sunbeam. The light streams in as long as the sun shines. And even when it's nighttime, we can remember that it will stream in again the next morning.

29. JUSTICE

An eye for an eye will make the whole world blind.
  - *Mohandas Gandhi*

Violet Cosmos

Justice: Metamorphoses

In the late '50s, psychologist Lawrence Kohlberg observed that as we mature, we progress through three basic levels of moral development. At the *pre-conventional* levels, our sense of what's fair and just is self-centered; we are concerned mainly with satisfying our own needs and avoiding punishment. Most of us move on to the *conventional* levels, where our sense of justice is based mainly on societal expectations; we make moral decisions based on rules, customs, and laws. Some reach the *post-conventional* levels, where principles and the desire for the greater good may take precedence over social norms and strictures. We move to the next level when we discover that the governing principles of our current level can no longer guide us. Then we are in new moral territory.

My own guiding principles have been challenged many times, but never as severely as they were in the aftermath of a successful medical malpractice trial in 1998. The story began with my nearly dying because of a series of medical errors five years earlier, continued with bringing the surgeon to trial, and took a bizarre turn when I discovered that the attorneys who won my case had absconded with the jury's award.

I had signed a release allowing my attorney, Jay, to deposit the check in his firm's escrow account, from which they were to pay me my share. I expected the award check to arrive soon after the trial ended. I spoke with Jay or his partner, Alan, every week or ten days, each time trying to pin down the date I would receive the money. They answered my direct questions with vague promises to "make some calls" and get back to me, reassuring me that delays were normal in cases like mine. "You have to trust your lawyer," Jay said, ending each call on a friendly note, suggesting we have a meal together or take in a movie at the Film Forum the next time I came to New York.

As the weeks passed, I grew frustrated and anxious. Two months after the trial, I still had not received my award. When I called the firm, their receptionist told me the office had flooded. She put me through to Alan, who explained that some of the records were water-logged and their computers may have been damaged. He assured me, though, that everything was still proceeding normally. I started to express my impatience and he quickly put Jay on the phone. "These things take time," Jay said. "You just need to be patient and stop being so anal about this, David. Your money's good as gold."

Another month went by. I called again, this time pressing hard for an exact date. Alan confessed that the reason for this latest delay was their fault. "I'm being honest with you," he said, "with all the mess after the flood, there's paperwork we forgot to put in." But I was not placated, and for the first time it dawned on me that my money might not be "good as gold" after all.

I realized something was seriously awry only after talking with the referring attorney, who told me that neither he nor our expert witnesses had been paid. "The big question," he said, "is why? Why would they throw away their expert witnesses? Why would they give up a stream of cases I could pass on to them? To me this makes sense only if they don't plan to be lawyers anymore."

"What do you mean?" I said.

"I think they're going to skip."

I contacted the firm that had defended the surgeon I'd sued. His attorney called the doctor's medical malpractice insurer, and they faxed me a copy of the award check. They'd mailed it out five days after the trial ended. Within minutes of receiving that fax, I decided to go to New York and demand my money. I spent the remainder of the morning writing a detailed complaint to send to the Manhattan D.A., the New York State Bar Association, and the federal, state, and city tax agencies.

I quickly packed a bag and then called a friend on the Upper East Side. "I'm either coming back with my money or I'm starting a shit storm," I told him. With the chilling sense that I was about to take a step after which there would be no turning back, I called their firm again.

"Oh, hello, Mr. Bookbinder, how are you?" the receptionist said. "What can I do for you?"

"You can tell your bosses that I'm meeting with them tomorrow morning at 10:00 a.m."

"Um... Do you want to talk to them?"

"No. Just give them that message. And tell them that if they don't make this meeting, they'll be getting calls from people they want to hear from even less than me."

She was silent for a moment, apparently writing down my message. "Less than you... Okay, sir. So, tomorrow at 10:00 a.m.?"

"Yeah. Just give them that message."

I printed duplicate copies of my complaint letters, put them in envelopes, and left one set on my desk for my girlfriend to mail if she didn't hear from me within two days. It was a melodramatic gesture, I knew, but at the time melodrama didn't seem entirely out of place. I grabbed my backpack and briefcase, a pocket knife I'd made years before, and a copy of Homer's *Odyssey*. On the commuter train to Boston, I turned to the section where Odysseus arrives home after his arduous journey, only to find that brutes have taken over his kingdom and squandered his fortune.

I had a regularly scheduled appointment with my therapist that afternoon, and I kept it. His office was decorated with Asian art and religious artifacts, as well as his own photographs, which strongly resembled oriental paintings. The meditative setting contrasted strongly with the fury inside me.

He noticed my backpack and gave it a quizzical nod. "I'm catching a bus to New York as soon as I leave here," I said. I filled him in on the events of the past week and explained what I planned to do when I got there. "My girlfriend thinks I'm crazy, but I feel like I need to do this. What do you think?"

Jim leaned back in his big, black leather chair and stroked his goatee. "I'm not sure I would go," he said. "It could be explosive."

"I'm not afraid of them," I said, though my heart was pounding. "What are they going to do, hire a hit man? Too many people already know about this." I took a breath to calm down. We talked about how helpful it had been to bring a collection of objects from friends and family to my medical malpractice trial. "I could use another set tomorrow," I said, "but there's no time." I took my homemade knife out of my pocket and handed it to him. "I did bring this, though, for luck."

Jim ran his fingers along the brass and ironwood exterior, then opened the knife and tested the blade on his fingertip before he passed it back. "It's a beautiful piece of work," he said. "Wait a minute. I have something for you." He reached over to a small altar near his desk and picked up a short silver dagger with a fluted, three-sided blade. "It's called a *phurba*," he explained. "It's one of the symbolic armaments Tibetan Buddhists use to deal with illusion." He handed it to me and I felt its unexpected heft. "It's a good image for you – the warrior with his sword of justice."

"I don't know if justice is what I'm after," I said. "What I want is vengeance. Those bastards tried to take my future. Whether they pay me or not, I'm going to take theirs. I'm an Old Testament Jew, Jim. We don't turn the other cheek."

It was not the first time we'd discussed revenge. "That's why I'm giving you the phurba," Jim said now. "It's the Dagger of Emptiness. You don't use it to attack your enemy; you use it to kill your own illusions." He waved a hand in front of his eyes. "The hero cuts away illusions – attachment, aversion, indifference – until all that's left is the truth. It's illusions that keep you feeling like a victim."

I shifted in my seat. "But I *am* a victim," I said. "That's the phrase, isn't it? 'A crime victim.' These are *bad guys*. They're probably hurting other people even as we speak. What's wrong with vengeance if it stops the bad guys?"

"In your shoes, I might feel the same way," Jim said. "Who wouldn't? But vengeance doesn't strengthen, it weakens. It comes from the rage of helplessness."

I fingered the phurba's soft, dull edges. "I've been re-reading the *Odyssey*, the last third. Odysseus is consumed with rage, and he acts on it with the blessing of the gods – slays the suitors who've taken over his kingdom, rivers of blood, and all that. Isn't he the archetypal hero?"

Jim shook his head. "Odysseus isn't the best model for what has to happen here. You don't have to slay the suitors. You have to slay the suitors within."

He told me a story of a young samurai whose master was murdered by an assassin. The samurai dedicated his life to tracking down the killer and bringing him to justice, finally cornering him in an alley halfway around the world. As the samurai drew his sword and prepared to take his enemy's head, the assassin spat in his face. The samurai paused, then sheathed his sword. The killer, shocked, said, "I murdered your master. I admit that now. Why do you not slay me?" The samurai replied, "For all these years I have been seeking justice. But when you spat at me, I became enraged. Then I was no longer a samurai upholding justice. I was just an angry man with a sword."

"The compassionate warrior doesn't act out of

vengeance," Jim said. "He sees his enemy as a diminished, tragic figure. You could say that these guys are winning because they seem to be getting away with robbery. But you can't be a person with no conscience and also experience everything that makes life worthwhile. Sociopaths like them are not whole human beings, and that's pitiable."

He took the phurba from me and stabbed toward his chest. "You can use this to help you direct your rage not at your enemies but at the forces in you that keep you from experiencing your true nature." He handed back the phurba. "Use it before you go in to talk to them tomorrow."

I thought about what he was saying, then put the phurba in my pocket. "Okay," I said. "I think I know what you mean."

"I know you do." He clapped me on the shoulder. "You may get your money or you may not, though I hope you do. These guys may be punished or they may not, though I hope they are. But whatever happens, if you stay on this path, you'll gain something that's worth a thousand times the money."

I looked at him skeptically. "What's that?"

"You'll throw off the chains of your victimhood. And nobody can take that away."

That afternoon, I took the bus to New York and, Jim's opinions about Odysseus notwithstanding, completed my re-reading of the *Odyssey*. I spent the night at my friend's place, then the following morning took the subway to the attorneys' midtown Manhattan offices. I was early and stopped in a diner for breakfast. In the restroom, I used the phurba as Jim had instructed. But on the way out, I also patted the pocket where my own knife lay, with its blade sharp enough to split a hair.

In a tense meeting with both attorneys, knife and phurba, Odysseus and samurai, struggled for control. I laid the envelopes I'd prepared on their conference table and stated my intentions. "Are you threatening us?" Jay said angrily.

"No," I said. "I'm just telling you what will happen if I don't get my money."

For most of the meeting I stayed firm in my resolve. Toward the end, though, I was won over by their claim that the IRS had frozen their escrow account, Alan's tearful plea not to "ruin our lives," and an offer of $10,000 on the spot, with more to come weekly until the end of the month, when, they assured me, I would be "made whole."

"I *am* whole," I said. "You're the ones who are broken." But I took the check.

I rode the bus back to Boston that afternoon feeling confused and uncertain, Jim's samurai tugging on one side, Odysseus on the other. A few days later I received another check for $5,000. I cashed it, but by then the samurai was gaining ground and I was starting to feel compromised. By the end of the month, there had been more pleas and more promises, but no more checks.

I contacted a local attorney, who stumbled on a Westchester County lawyer who represented another of my attorneys' clients. I learned that her funds, too, had been "delayed." That confirmed my suspicions that I was not unique and tipped the balance in favor of the samurai. I knew I had to stop them. I mailed the complaint letters to the Manhattan D.A., the New York State Bar Association, and the tax agencies, and let the judicial system begin its process. As I dropped the envelopes into the mailbox, the veil of confusion lifted.

By the time I testified before the grand jury a year later, the samurai and Odysseus had reached détente. The following year, when I read a statement at my attorneys' sentencing hearing, I no longer desired revenge, but only for them to be separated from people they would otherwise continue to harm. On that day in court, as I looked at these formerly high-flying men standing before the judge in their orange jump suits, I felt, unbidden, the faintest glimmerings of pity and the barest intimations of compassion.

The legal term my attorneys had used, "made whole," means "to pay or award damages sufficient to put the party who was damaged back into the position he/she would have been without the fault of another." It seems apt in a larger sense. In the weeks following my turning them in, I gained a sense of wholeness, of no longer being the victim of the surgeon, the attorneys, or anyone else. I moved on, changed in ways that, as Jim predicted, nothing has taken away.

30. LISTENING

The first duty of love is to listen.
   - *Paul Tillich*

Rudbeckia 'Prairie Sun'

LISTENING: SELF, OTHERS

Failures to listen are endemic to our species.

The most common complaint from parents who bring their children to me for counseling is that "they don't listen," by which the parent usually means that the child does not obey. When I talk with children, they likewise complain that their parents don't listen, but they mean it literally. Failure to listen to children has subtle but enduring consequences. Kids who grow up unheard can pass on what they experienced to their own children.

I discovered the value of listening carefully to children, in their words and their behaviors, many years ago. One evening, while visiting one of my brothers, I joined the family for a dinner of fried chicken. My niece, then three years old, repeatedly asked for "an angel." My brother and his wife told her to stop complaining and eat her dinner. As her requests for "an angel" became more strident, so did her parents' reprimands. I found myself wondering what she might mean by "an angel" and offered her a chicken wing. She smiled, took the wing, and happily finished her meal.

The complaints I hear from couples are similar to those I hear from parents: "He doesn't listen." "She doesn't listen." "He/she did it for no reason." But there is *always* a reason; usually, we need only to ask, and to listen, to determine what it is.

Many of us are so concerned with what we want to say, or so convinced that our beliefs are true, that instead of really listening, we talk over one another, interrupt, discard the other person's point of view, leaving unheard and often unspoken the deeper parts of who we are.

In the Buddhist sangha I attend, each week someone reads from the writings of a teacher. The teachings are called the *dharma*, and we explore them in a dharma discussion. One by one, as we are so moved, we speak either to the topic of the reading or to something important that has occurred in our lives. A sangha rule is that after someone speaks, we wait three slow breaths before anyone else talks, so we have time to fully take in what each of us has shared. We don't need to mentally rehearse anything, we don't have to look for the right time to chime in, and we aren't afraid that we won't have a chance to say what we need to say. There is, somehow, always enough time.

With my niece, I was outside the family system and could see the dynamic from a distance. As a therapist, I am also outside the family system and can sometimes discern, more readily than its members, where communication has broken down. And, as a sangha member, I am reminded of how to listen at the beginning of each dharma discussion. But we don't have to be outside the family system, or therapists, or Buddhists, to listen. We just have to practice.

The following exercises are some I have found helpful in my training and my life. You might, too. They are all practiced by two people. First, one speaks while the other listens, and then they reverse roles. You may wish to try them with a friend or family member.

1. Listen silently. Sit quietly for five minutes and listen to someone talk about something important. Signal your interest using only your facial expressions and your eyes.

2. Listen with tonal responses. Add, to the above, non-verbal utterances such as "Ah!" "Mmm," "Uh-huh," and so on.

3. Listen with body language. Add, to the above, by responding to the body language of the speaker with your own body language.

4. Listen with comments on tonal responses and body language. Add, to the above, by commenting on the speaker's tone and body language, but *not* on his or her words. "I noticed your voice dropped." "I see that you're shaking your head from side to side."

5. Listen with mirroring. Finally, add to the other exercises by directly mirroring what the speaker says. Listen to what feels like a chunk of monologue and then signal the speaker to pause. Next, say something like, "So, it sounds to me as if you are saying.... Is that right?" If you have captured the gist of what the speaker said, the speaker continues with the next chunk. If not, the speaker clarifies, then you mirror back the clarification to make sure that you now understand.

By nature, we may not be good listeners. But, *by nature* we are not good at many things, and yet we eventually learn to do them well. Listening skills are not complex and they are easily learned. Even young children I have worked with can become quite skillful at listening, often with surprisingly little instruction. So can we all.

31. LONGING

We can never give up longing and wishing while we are thoroughly alive. There are certain things we feel to be beautiful and good, and we must hunger after them.

- *George Eliot*

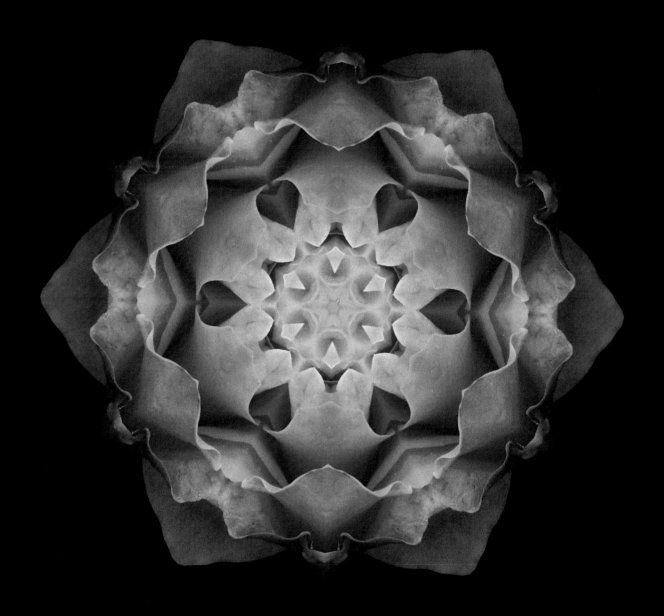

Pink Fall Rose

LONGING: INCLINATIONS

A writer I knew some years ago collected her poems into a book she planned to call *The Color of Longing*. My own longings have come in many colors and many shades: longing for love, longing for knowledge, longing for peace both within myself and on the planet, longing to create truly beautiful work, longing for a career that feels purposeful.

Longing can feel like a painful kind of pining, but without longing there would be little new in our lives. Longing propels us in the direction organisms need to go. Much as a flower inclines toward the light, so longing can move us out of our complacency, our comfortable discomfort, into the gap between where we are and where we long to be. It is within this gap that meaningful change becomes possible.

When I was a teenager, I read a collection of science fiction stories set in a future where all people are telepathically connected. Some were natural telepaths, while others used machines designed to link minds to minds, hearts to hearts, memories and thoughts to memories and thoughts. The narrator, a badly wounded survivor of a helicopter crash, loses this connection when his telepathic device is damaged in the accident. To keep from being driven mad by the anguish of sudden isolation, he retells the stories of his race, beginning with the first, persecuted, telepathic mutants. Though he is near death when his rescuers finally arrive, the first thing they do is reconnect him to the telepathic device.

Back then, I also was isolated, but only while reading these stories did I became conscious of my separation. Resonating with the narrator made me feel my aloneness, and, like the injured pilot, I began to long for connection, too. This longing inclined me, for the next 35 years, to a series of occupations — writing, teaching, counseling — that increasingly stretched my connection boundaries. Over the decades, longing has continued to motivate me to expand and open my heart.

For most of my adult life I have been conscious, as well, of a spiritual longing, and it has compelled me to explore many religious practices and the depths of my soul. Since my early 20s I've been especially drawn to Buddhism and Sufism and at one juncture received a Sufi name. It is a seeker's name and translates roughly to "One who longs for the Beloved."

Now I wonder if, perhaps, *everything* longs for the Beloved.

French philosopher, paleontologist, and Jesuit priest Tielhard de Chardin, one of the discoverers of Peking Man, believed that the universe is evolving toward increasing complexity and consciousness, drawn by a supreme source he called the Omega Point, synonymous with God.

I've often pondered how self-aware species such as ours fit into the grand scheme of the universe. Why, I wonder, have we for so long been driven to build, and in particular to build increasingly complex artifacts that extend us physically and mentally? Our building and extending seems both purposeful and inevitable. I think it is only a matter of time before what we build reaches sufficient complexity to achieve sentience, and that as we continue to push out from our blue marble, extending our boundaries ever deeper into the cosmos, we will take this new sentience with us.

I hope that other sentient beings, on other worlds, are engaged in similar endeavors, drawn to the Omega Point by their own longings, continually extending themselves and their reach. I can imagine a day when our Earthbound intelligences, both organic and inorganic, will reach across the chasm between the stars and connect with other sentient beings. If, as de Chardin hypothesized, the evolution of the universe is incited by a ubiquitous longing for the Beloved, then perhaps our role is to become the nervous system of the great body of our universe as it slowly realizes its single, integrating consciousness and at last joins with the object of its longing.

32. LOVE

The gaze of love is not deluded. Love sees what is best
in the beloved, even when what is best in the beloved
finds it hard to emerge into the light.

  - J. M. Coetzee

Red Beach Rose

LOVE: ESSENTIALS

When I was 25, living in Manhattan, and trying to jump-start a career in writing and photography, I visited my parents and brothers in Buffalo two or three times a year. On those trips, I also saw my maternal grandmother.

It was painful to witness Bubby's decline. Though only in her mid 70s, by then she was legally blind, mostly deaf, unable to manage on her own. She had a room at a Jewish nursing home downtown, an institutional environment where I always felt uneasy.

On one visit, as I was leaving I noticed two of Bubby's former neighbors sitting in folding chairs on the lawn. I went over to them. Mr. Klein's recent stroke had paralyzed one side of his body and frozen half his face; his attempts to talk were unintelligible. Mrs. Klein, however, seemed virtually unchanged since I'd last seen her, more than ten years before. She asked how I was and what I was doing. I described my hoped-for journalism career and told her about my girlfriend, with whom I had briefly lived after college, and whom I had followed to New York. Our relationship was difficult, I told Mrs. Klein, "but I love her."

"Love?" Mrs. Klein said, gesturing toward her crippled husband. She looked me in the eyes. "Love is 50 years."

In that moment my concept of love changed permanently.

There Mrs. Klein was, content to be living in a place I found disturbing even to visit, because that's where her husband needed to be. I understood that for her, love wasn't about sex or passion, or getting what she needed, or even conversation. Nor was it about soul mates, shared interests, "chemistry," or any of the other things I sought in a relationship. Instead, it was about setting aside her needs for the sake of another and feeling no resentment.

Unless I somehow beat even the most wildly optimistic predictions for life expectancy, I will never approach Mrs. Klein's 50 years with one person. But I have long reflected on that conversation, and in the decades since then I've been learning to embrace what she was trying to teach me. Through a much different path, I have come to a similar place: to see that love is about recognizing the essential humanity of the other person *in toto* and responding to it with an open heart.

In his poem "New Heaven and Earth," D. H. Lawrence wrote about crossing over from a world "tainted with myself" into "a new world." Before his crossing, "I was a lover. I kissed the woman I loved, and God of horror, I was kissing also myself. I was a father and begetter of children, and oh, oh horror, I was begetting and conceiving in my own body." Afterward, when he reaches out in the night and touches his wife's side, he experiences her not as an extension of himself, but as "she who is the other." When we experience others as truly *other*, with their own needs, wants, and desires, we can begin the process of fully loving them.

Love need not even be requited. In the surrealistic movie *Adaptation*, based on the novel *The Orchid Thief*, Nicholas Cage portrays twin brothers, Charles and Donald Kaufman. Toward the end of the film, both brothers are pinned down in a swamp at gunpoint by the author of the novel (played by Meryl Streep) and her lover. Facing death, Charles tells Donald a secret he has been keeping since high school: He'd often seen his brother flirting with a girl who seemed kind and sweet when she was with Donald, but made fun of him with her friends as soon as he was out of earshot. To spare Donald's feelings, Charles had kept this to himself all those years.

"I heard them," Donald says.

"How come you looked so happy?" Charles asks.

"I loved Sarah, Charles," Donald says. "It was mine, that love. I owned it. Even Sarah didn't have the right to take it away."

"She thought you were pathetic."

"That was her business, not mine. You are what you love, not what loves you," Donald says.

Being a therapist has helped me to practice loving selflessly. Therapeutic love is about seeing and accepting the essential nature of someone, what pioneer psychologist Carl Rogers called "unconditional positive regard," and then reflecting it back, if necessary holding it for safekeeping when the object of that love can't yet take it in. It is the foundation of the best therapeutic relationships, a love seldom directly stated and also, I believe, one that's necessary for any truly healing relationship.

Like Donald's love in *Adaptation*, selfless love asks for nothing in return, and it does not end when the beloved is gone. The love itself lives on.

33. MIRACLES

There are two ways to live: You can live as if nothing
is a miracle; you can live as if everything is a miracle.

  - *Albert Einstein*

Dandelion

MIRACLES: YELLOW BRICK ROADS

I am a miracle worker by trade. Or more precisely, a facilitator of miracles.

I state this with humility. My powers are as ordinary as those of the Wizard of Oz, whose only real magic was tricking Dorothy, the Tin Woodsman, the Scarecrow, and the Cowardly Lion into beginning a journey out of their self-limiting beliefs.

The best trick I've found to facilitate miracles is deceptively simple. (Like the Wizard, I, too, sometimes need to be a little deceptive). It's called the Miracle Question and it goes like this:

Imagine that after you finish this essay you do whatever you would normally do with the rest of today. But tonight, while you're asleep, a strange thing happens: A miracle occurs. This miracle is just for you, and it's that all your problems and concerns are solved. Wonderful, right? However, there's a catch. Because the miracle happened while you were asleep, when you wake up tomorrow, you're in the world of the miracle from here on out, but you don't know it. So the question is: What do you notice, from the moment you wake up and as you step through your day, that eventually gets you thinking, "Something's different about today. A miracle must have happened!"

You are looking for a shift in awareness like Dorothy's after the tornado deposited her in Oz. She steps out of her house, looks around, and, as the film itself shifts into Technicolor, she sees the yellow brick road, the horse of many colors, the munchkins. She turns to her little dog and exclaims, "Toto, I've a feeling we're not in Kansas anymore!" You are looking for what leads you to your I'm-not-in-Kansas-anymore moment.

The Miracle Question is part of Solution-Focused therapy, which is based on the belief that all of us have the means to solve our own problems. The question helps people to envision, while in a guided visualization, what their lives can be when all their current concerns have been addressed and issues resolved.

After I ask clients the Miracle Question, I lead them through answering it, using prompts like: *How do you feel when you open your eyes? Are you in the same bedroom? The same house? With the same people? What's different as you get ready for the day? What's different as you step through it, hour by hour? What do other people in your life notice about you that's different? What do you notice about them?*

Gradually, as they walk through their miracle day, a detailed vision of that different life emerges. Then it's just a matter of working toward the miracle, one doable step at a time.

After clients have answered the Miracle Question, they reflect on what pieces of the miracle are already part of their lives, in whole or in part. Then I ask them to evaluate their present life on a scale of 1–10, where "1" is how things were when they were as far away from the miracle as they have ever been, and "10" is they are living the miracle 24/7. The number they come up with is where their journey begins.

Before they leave the session, clients decide on a task or experiment that they hope will move them closer to their miracle. The choice is important. Generally, it shouldn't be something they would do anyway, nor should it be so daunting that they won't attempt it. Instead, the best experiment is something they really want to do, even if there is some anxiety, and they believe that regardless of the outcome, just doing it will raise their score. At our next meeting, we look at what happened and make course corrections as needed. Then we repeat the process until, step by step, week by week, they create their miracle.

It is difficult to get somewhere if you don't know your destination and have no way to check that you're on the right path. Answering the Miracle Question helps us envision the desired destination, the experiments move us forward, and the 1–10 scaling provides a means for verifying that we're still on track.

The Miracle Question is like the Call to Adventure that launches the Hero's Journey. It impels us to take risks and endure struggles we might not otherwise have taken and endured, but which yield rewards that cannot be obtained any other way. Much as Dorothy discovered she always had a home, the Tin Woodsman found his compassion, the Scarecrow displayed his brilliance, and the Lion showed his courage, by traversing our own yellow brick roads, we become who we are meant to be.

Perhaps today is when you begin a journey down *your* yellow brick road. What will you notice when you wake up tomorrow?

34. MISTAKES

The events we bring upon ourselves, no matter how
unpleasant, are necessary in order to learn what we
need to learn.

- *Richard Bach*

White Beach Rose

Mistakes: Alchemy

Many of my older clients come to therapy feeling disturbed by what they see as lost opportunities, wrong choices, wasted years. Even my younger clients, some only in their mid-20s, often compare themselves to their peers and find their own lives wanting – they've missed the boat, time and opportunity have gone on without them, they will never catch up. As they describe the mistakes they have made, they turn their faces downward, their eyes sometimes glistening with tears, tones of anguish or bitterness in their voices. What emanates from them is regret and shame.

They may have rationalized that "everything happens for a reason," but they only half believe it; what possible good has come from these bad decisions, these preventable losses? Or perhaps their friends and families have attempted to console them by explaining, "You didn't know what you didn't know." But this truism seldom provides relief because they can often retort, "But I did know! I knew it was a mistake and I did it anyway!"

I, too, have a catalog of such mistakes: Relationships that I knew early on could not work but held onto anyway, hoping against hope. More than a decade of toiling away as a tech writer when I knew I should have been writing something else. Disastrous financial errors anyone with common sense would have avoided. Medical decisions that nearly got me killed. The list is long.

I understand my clients' feelings of shame and regret and the anger they direct at themselves. But in recent years I have also, mostly, moved past these emotions. I have found that mistakes, while I may wish I had never made them, have redeeming qualities and (as a former girlfriend once said about me and *my* redeeming qualities), they *are* redeeming.

When I talk to clients about their regrets and their shame, I encourage them to avoid the trap of victimhood, to see obstacles, even those they have created themselves, as challenges. Mistakes become, in the words of another old friend, "just another AFGO." Introducing this acronym (**A**nother **F***ing **G**rowth **O**pportunity) generally gets a laugh, but it also articulates a grudging acceptance that helps us see the possibilities of positive change that can emerge from negative experiences – even from our mistakes.

I'm fortunate in having been guided to a profession where my personal mistakes can often be redeemed not only by learning from them, but also by being able to pass on to others what I have figured out.

Mistakes in my own relationships have enabled me to help clients refocus marriages that have gone awry, or to end those that have lingered for years in a barely tolerable state. An unanticipated benefit of drifting from one career to another has been understanding firsthand the many different contexts my clients work in, and helping them to see other directions they, too, might take, if the current path has become a dead end.

When it's clear that one of my mistakes echoes a client's, I may talk about what I've done, what I have lost, and what I eventually gained. "Maybe I can save you some time and trouble," I might add. When it seems appropriate, I describe the mistakes that led to my becoming a therapist, and how I continue to mine them for the growth opportunities they contain.

I also speak about the Hero's Journey and how, in many of the tales of heroism handed down for centuries, the protagonists make bad decisions, but their mistakes turn out to be a necessary part of their journey from being not-quite-a-hero to becoming truly heroic. This arc shows up even in comedies such as the movie *Groundhog Day*, in which the weather man protagonist, played by Bill Murray, is trapped in a single 24-hour period. He literally makes the same mistakes over and over, unable to continue to the next day until he starts to experiment, to learn, to grow as a person, and finally to be free, as a transformed and more authentic version of himself, to awaken on February 3rd and go on with the rest of his life.

Each time I am able to help someone by using insights I would not have had if I'd avoided making mistakes, my own errors become less painful. They feel more like small sacrifices I unwittingly made for the sake of others I was yet to meet. This process is alchemical, turning the lead in my life into gold, so that I can give it away.

35. NEEDS

You attract everything you need and most of what you want.

- *Fortune cookie*

Violet Dahlia

NEEDS: DEMONS, ALLIES, SHADOWS

Sometimes the things that plague us seem demonic. Helplessly, we watch as we act in ways we know are not good for us. But no matter how hard we try to stop, our demons keep egging us on. If only we could exorcise them....

Of course, we're not really possessed. Most of us engage in negative behaviors because we have unmet, and often unconscious, needs. These unmet needs turn into "wants." We "want" to put things off, get drunk, get mad. Our true needs, however, are only indirectly met by satisfying these wants.

Our wants are often motivated by what therapists call "secondary gains," hidden benefits of self-defeating or self-destructive behaviors. Secondary gains can show up very early – for example, in children who "act out" in school because they have an unmet need for positive attention, and negative attention is better than none. Other examples include underachieving, when we don't try our hardest because we fear the shame of failing to meet expectations; some forms of disability, when patients ignore the advice of their doctors because being injured protects them from the stresses of their previous lives; and addiction, when, even as their lives fall apart, addicts continue to get high to achieve temporary respite from trauma, regret, guilt, or shame.

When we recognize the negative impact of pursuing our wants, we usually try to reform. We resolve to stop drinking, be on time, control our anger, get things done. But stories such as *Dr. Jekyll and Mr. Hyde* demonstrate what is evident in our own lives: Our shadow sides can't simply be controlled, suppressed, or eliminated. Denying our wants only makes our demons more determined. They persist not because they are trying to destroy us, but to try to help us meet our needs. Although their methods are ineffective, their intentions are usually positive. To meet our true needs, we can embrace our demons instead of trying to defeat them.

An ancient Tibetan practice called *chöd* can uncover the needs beneath our demons' wants and convert our demons into allies. The practice, as taught by author and teacher Lama Tsultrim Allione, can be performed in about half an hour.[1]

Begin by arranging two chairs so they face each other and you can move easily from one to the other. Then perform these steps:

1. Find the demon. Close your eyes and scan your body. Become aware of sensations and feelings you associate with your demon. Imagine them as colors, shapes, textures, temperatures, smells, and sounds.

2. Personify the demon. With your eyes still closed, envision the sensations you are recalling as a demon sitting opposite you. Notice how it looks. Pay special attention to the expression in its eyes. Ask it a) what it wants from you, b) what it needs from you, and c) how it will feel when it gets what it needs.

3. Become the demon. Eyes still closed, change places with the demon by moving to the opposite chair. Settle into your demon's identity and visualize your normal self sitting in the other chair. As the demon, answer the three questions you asked it. In your answers, distinguish carefully between "wants" and "needs." For instance, an addict demon may *want* drugs, but may *need* relief. When it gets this relief, it may feel calm and peaceful.

4. Feed the demon, meet the ally. Change places again, eyes closed. Imagine separating your consciousness from your body, then let your body melt into a nectar consisting of what the demon will feel when it gets what it needs. Feed this nectar to the demon and watch as the demon transforms.

When it has absorbed all it can, the demon may change to another form or disappear. If it transforms, ask the transformed demon if it is an ally. If it is, ask the ally a) how it will serve you, b) what commitment it will make to you, c) how it will protect you, and d) how you can access to it. If it isn't an ally, or if the demon has disappeared, then call an ally to appear and ask the ally the same four questions.

Change places. Become the ally and answer the questions. Change places for the last time and, in your original chair, settle back into yourself. Imagine you are getting the help the ally has offered. Feel the ally and you become one, then let yourself dissolve into emptiness.

5. Rest in awareness. Rest, taking a break from the thinking mind, experiencing open awareness.

Chöd incorporates into one exercise several techniques modern psychotherapy has rediscovered. My clients have often felt liberated by it, and practicing chöd has been an important component of my own reintegration and healing.

[1] Adapted from *Feeding Your Demons: Ancient Wisdom for Resolving Inner Conflict*, by Tsultrim Allione.

36. PATH

If a man does not keep pace with his companions, perhaps it is because he hears a different drummer. Let him step to the music which he hears, however measured or far away.

 - *Henry David Thoreau*

White Clematis

PATH: WITH HEART

Many years ago, I visited my brother Mark and his family near the capital of the tiny country of Luxembourg. One evening, I borrowed Mark's car and went into the town square to meet an American friend of his for dinner. She and I spent several hours together, exploring the sights and sampling the night life. It was after midnight when we parted. As I turned to head home, I realized I had no idea how to find the car.

I'd parked during the day and entered what I had assumed was the main gate into the square, but now I saw that there were a dozen entrances, and in the dark I couldn't tell which one I'd taken. I didn't speak any of the languages native to Luxembourg, and anyway, there were very few people around who could have helped me. For several minutes, I froze in the middle of the square, unable to choose a direction. All I remembered was that I'd parked near water.

If you don't know where a path goes, it's hard to take the first step.

After the 2008 financial crash, many of the people I saw in therapy were confused. They'd lost jobs, moved out of apartments or houses that were now beyond their means, and been forced to examine where they'd been, what had changed, and where they might go from there.

I still encounter clients in this state, and I often ask them to do what a former therapist asked me to do when I was similarly adrift. I'd returned to Boston after four years in a PhD program in English and realized I no longer wanted to be an English professor. He suggested I make a list of everything I ever liked to do, still liked doing, or would like to do in the future, and bring it to our next session. The following week, we sorted the list. Many of my "likes" fit into just five categories: seeing (literally and metaphorically), figuring things out, helping people, fixing things, and teaching. We looked for occupations that combined at least two. It wasn't a stretch to see that working as a psychotherapist encompassed most of them.

When I do this exercise with clients, the result is often a return to a nearly forgotten dream. Something buried under depression, anxiety, hardship, or family expectations breaks through, and interests from long ago

get re-activated. Then, clients start to forge a new path that's a better fit for their talents and joys. But the road to self-actualization is not always clear, and taking a few steps down several paths may be the only way to find out which one is right for you; which, as Carlos Casteneda put it in *The Teachings of Don Juan*, is "a path with heart."

On that evening in Luxembourg, I learned that going down the "wrong" path is sometimes the only way to get anywhere at all. After my brief panic, I remembered that it was about a 10-minute walk from the car to where I'd previously entered the square. If I took any exit and walked *11* minutes without seeing the car, I reasoned, I would know I'd taken the wrong one. If so, I could double back to the square and try again. In the worst case, I might make all the wrong choices before selecting the correct exit, but I'd still find the car in a little over four hours.

I found it on the third try.

Many of us are poised on the brink of a new direction but remain frozen at a crossroads of possibilities and risks, afraid to venture down *any* path because we might make the wrong choice. Instead, we ponder and research and fret, but we can't decide: there are too many unknowns. To get anywhere, we need to start down *some* path, if only to rule it out. And once we are in motion, we need to discern whether the path we are on is one with heart.

The closing statement of the Buddhist sangha I belong to goes like this:

> *This day is ended. Our lives are shorter. Now we look carefully at what we have done. Let us live deeply, free from affliction, aware of impermanence, so that life does not drift by, squandered.*

When we are on a path with heart, the going may be no easier than when we are on another path. But we don't mind. We sense that we are not just passing time because we can feel the path taking us where we need to go. And when we come to the end of our days, we know that our time on the planet has not been squandered.

I don't think it gets any better than that.

37. PATIENCE

Patience is also a form of action.
  - *Auguste Rodin*

White Cosmos

PATIENCE: PRACTICE

Motorcycle maintenance has always been an important part of riding for me. Knowing more than just the basics gives me confidence that I can get the bike going if it breaks down on the highway, and it also helps me feel connected to the machine.

I used to be good at it. Back in the mid '70s, on a long road trip, I seized a piston climbing a steep hill in Ohio. I managed to break it free, limp to Chicago, and drag the bike into a friend's basement. There, with only the tools in my tool kit and a few from a borrowed tool box, I disassembled the engine. Then I got the cylinder bored out, replaced the damaged piston with a larger one, and rode the bike another thousand miles home.

When I started riding again after a very long hiatus, I soon found I'd forgotten most of what I'd known about motorcycle maintenance. The learning curve for returning to riding was steep, but I climbed it in four days. The curve for motorcycle maintenance, however, has been much tougher to surmount. Some of what I once knew is coming back, but I still have a long way to go.

One of my main obstacles to becoming proficient at motorcycle maintenance has been lack of patience. I took a leap forward, however, when I watched how my engineer brother, Mark, approaches this task.

Mark and I converge on Syracuse in the late spring and early fall to visit our mother and to ride together with my brother Paul. On one such trip, Mark, who is not only a mechanical engineer but also a motorcycle safety instructor, volunteered to help me adjust my motorcycle engine's valves.

My bike is an old single-cylinder design and its four valves need adjusting every 5,000 miles. When I looked up the procedure in the repair manual, accessing the valves seemed straightforward, but manipulating a feeler gauge, a wrench, and a screw driver in the cramped space available felt too daunting for me even to attempt. But it was not daunting to Mark, who has an engineer's confidence that if one man can design a piece of machinery, another can maintain it.

His first try at adjustment was unsuccessful. He couldn't even get the feeler gauge in place. When that happened, I felt my body tense up and my jaw tighten – I was 350 miles from home and the bike was now unrideable. But instead of panicking like me, Mark stepped away from the machine, seemed to reset himself emotionally, and reflected on what he'd learned from this attempt. Then he came at it again, bending the feeler gauge so it more easily reached the gap. That was better, but there was a problem with the adjustment nut. So he stepped back again, reset himself, and again reflected on what he had learned. On the third try, he got it, and he quickly adjusted the remaining valves using the technique he'd devised.

Riding back from Syracuse on my freshly tuned bike, I thought about my brother's approach: Make an attempt, and if it doesn't succeed, reset yourself, incorporate what you learned, and try again. Then rinse, lather, and repeat as needed. This methodology, I realized, epitomized patience.

Patience applies to much more than working on mechanical devices. Without patience, qualities such as forgiveness, resilience, and opportunity are all difficult, if not impossible, to realize. Patience with ourselves and others allows us to forgive. Patience with loss permits us, little by little, to overcome it. Patience with opportunity helps us both to see it when it arrives and, when it does not, to be open to it in the future.

Psychotherapy, too, is a patience practice. Week after week, clients struggle with the same issues, and it would be easy for both me and the client to throw up our hands in frustration. But instead, we go down a path of potential healing together, continue along it as far as seems helpful, and when we hit a block, we reset, reevaluate, and then start down another.

Opportunities for developing patience present themselves every day. Even small, regular tasks can be our teachers: cleaning the bathroom, washing the dishes, dealing with traffic on the commute to work. Lessons learned from approaching these tasks in a patient, mindful way can transfer to our more formidable challenges.

When I was a college student, the phrase "Don't push the river, it flows by itself" became a meme. At the time, I thought it was synonymous with "Go with the flow." But now I see it as encouraging patience. Whether that river is the congested highway at rush hour or the temporal currents that draw us toward the ends of our lives, we don't need to push it. With patience, we can let it carry us along.

38. PERCEPTION

If the doors of perception were cleansed every thing
would appear to man as it is, infinite.

For man has closed himself up, till he sees all things
thro' narrow chinks of his cavern.

  - *William Blake*

White Begonia

PERCEPTION: DISPELLING

Many of us go through our lives under the enchantment of a Spell.

This Spell is not cast by sorcerers. Instead, we create it from unconscious messages we received as children about ourselves and others, and it comprises the thoughts, feelings, and behaviors we developed to protect us from harm. Our Spells, as described by psychologist Jim Grant, helped us navigate our early lives, but later they constrain us like tight-fitting shoes we have outgrown. They become a grid through which everything else is perceived, and they can shield us from experiences, relationships, and challenges that foster self-actualization.

For instance, a boy born into a working-class family might learn by example that he'll be a blue-collar worker when he grows up. Despite straight A's in school and the observations of teachers and guidance counselors that he has a great aptitude for math and should go to college, he becomes a factory worker like his father and grandfather before him. Or the daughter of authoritarian parents, instructed to "stop being a baby" whenever she cries or asks for help, learns to withhold her feelings and to see herself as strong and independent. But as she grows up, she may be unable to break through barriers to intimacy she does not even know are there.

Breaking our Spells opens our eyes to who we truly are and enables us to more fully emerge. Though they are powerful, Spells are much like computer programs, in that they follow a set pattern, and that is their weakness. To break them, we must recognize, challenge, and interrupt them.

Spell patterns. Accurately perceiving our patterns is the first step in Spell breaking. If, for example, we have been in a series of unsatisfying romantic relationships, we can find the common denominators in the people we have chosen and the relationships we've had with them, and choose a different type of person and a different way to be in relationship. If we are in an unsatisfying career, we can look at what led us to the work we've done and the environment we've chosen and make different choices moving forward. We may not get our next steps exactly right, but we have a far better chance of doing so than when our perceptions are distorted by unconscious patterns.

Spell voice. Many of us use a particular tone and vernacular when we describe habitual conflicts or speak in the voice of our inner critics. These are our Spell voices. Often Spells use the familiar voice of a family or community member who had some power over us as children and who, by proxy, continues to exert that power internally. Recognizing this voice clues us to its source.

Spell vocabulary. Our Spells tend to use carefully selected words and phrases, incantations that interfere with our efforts to awaken. Each of us has our own Spell vocabulary, but some words are common to many Spells. They are like the "tells" that give poker players away. For example, if we catch ourselves using the word "just" multiple times in a paragraph – "I *just* did it because…," or "I *just* don't care…," or "I'm *just* tired of…" – we can suspect the Spell of clouding our judgment to hide its handiwork. When we feel "overwhelmed," we can surmise that the Spell is trying to convince us to turn back from what could actually be a path to liberation.

Spell beliefs. Fundamental to Spell-breaking is recognizing Spell beliefs about ourselves, others, and how we should act. These are subliminal messages that tend to limit our actions to those that continue our Spells. Most of us have only a few of these beliefs, and identifying them goes a long way toward dislodging the Spell. Misperceptions and the mistaken beliefs they generate can often be readily disproved when we challenge them.

Spell allies. A critical component of Spell-breaking is perceiving who, in our circles of friends, family, and associates, is an ally of our true selves, and who reinforces our Spells. We may need to redefine our relationships with Spell allies – or end them. We may need to build new relationships with people who support our true selves.

Once we see through our Spell's illusions, we get better at challenging them. We recognize Spell vocabulary and catch the Spell before it deceives us. We lessen the hold of Spell beliefs by exposing and disputing them. We break Spell patterns by choosing to do something else. We resist Spell commands by considering their source: Has it ever been a trustworthy guide?

Our true selves and our Spells share the same energy. When we interrupt the Spell's program, it weakens and we grow stronger. When we interrupt it often enough, it loses its power entirely, setting us free.

39. PERFECTION

The Perfect is the enemy of the Good.

- *Voltaire*

Purple Echinacea

Perfection: Antidotes

My father was a storekeeper and the son of working-class immigrants. He wanted his children to do better than he had, and he believed the gateway to a successful life was education. Consequently, he held me, his firstborn, to high academic standards. This meant I had to get A's, and to earn my father's approval I abandoned many other activities so I could focus on schoolwork. By the time I completed high school, I had achieved a perfect average and was class valedictorian, but I'd learned very little about many other important aspects of life.

The roots of the drive for perfection are spread wide and go deep. The ancient Greeks saw perfection as necessary for beauty and high art. Buddhists are encouraged to practice the Six Perfections as part of the path to enlightenment. St. Matthew exhorted, "Be ye therefore perfect even as your Father which is in heaven is perfect."

Our culture's idealization of perfection extends beyond religion, philosophy, and art. Our leaders should be perfect (George Washington never told a lie, Abe Lincoln walked miles to return a penny). The media projects images of perfect skin, perfect hair, perfect teeth, perfect bodies, and perfect lives, and offers us products to attain them.

Many of us see perfectionism as a motivator. Certainly, striving for excellence has characterized people who have made important contributions in the arts, sciences, philosophy, law, spirituality, athletics, and many other fields. But striving for excellence and perfectionism are not synonymous. Those who strive for excellence do their best and see setbacks as challenges, defeats as learning opportunities. Perfectionists, on the other hand, get their self-esteem from "perfect" behavior, appearance, and accomplishments. When they fail to achieve a goal or to conform to often unrealistic standards, they feel defective and ashamed.

Perfectionists are more often paralyzed, not motivated, by perfectionism. They can be plagued by envy when they see someone doing "better" than they're doing, or they can languish in a state of potential, hating themselves for failing to achieve anything "important" but unable to choose a path because they might be unsuccessful.

A less extreme symptom of perfectionism afflicts people who avoid being seen in public unless their appearance is "perfect." When they do find a spot on their clothing, a mark on their face, or some other "defect," they may spend hours, even days, reviewing every contact they had that day, worrying that someone might have noticed this "imperfection."

If you see a tendency toward perfectionism – you work too hard at something that may be impossible, worry excessively about how others might perceive you, beat yourself up for minor missteps, avoid challenges because you're afraid you won't handle them perfectly – try the following:

1. Record the thought. Write a sentence that captures your basic perfectionistic belief. For example, "If I'm not perfect, I am nothing," or "If I make a mistake, I'll lose everything."

2. Question the belief. Is this belief always true, not only for you but also for other people? Where did this belief come from? Does it contribute to your well-being?

3. Create an affirmation. Create a counter-statement that more accurately describes your reality. Effective affirmations ring true, but they come from a gentler, more sympathetic place. For example, if you catch yourself thinking "If I'm not perfect, I'm nothing," you can substitute an affirmation such as "I don't have to be perfect to be loved and happy." If your initial try at an affirmation doesn't feel credible, change it to something that does. For instance, "I'm not perfect, but I'm still okay, and I'm working on getting better" carries a hint of perfectionism, but it also has an optimistic spin. A little different is enough to disrupt the perfectionist pattern and make an opening for change.

The ultimate antidote to perfectionism is self-acceptance. Self-acceptance is taking stock of things as they are and allowing them to *just be*. It is letting go of strivings, regrets, and self-recrimination. It is saying, "Whatever is, is. Whatever has been, has been. This is who and where I am now." With self-acceptance, we can comfortably follow Ralph Waldo Emerson's advice: "Finish each day and be done with it. You have done what you could."

Those of us who tend toward perfectionism may not want to give it up entirely. Choosing to do a few things "perfectly" can be satisfying in ways that trying to wholly conform to perfectionistic standards is not. For example, I freely indulge my desire to keep my computer functioning "perfectly" and to tinker with a photograph until it's "perfect." I know that perfecting these things takes more of the limited time I have on the planet than is really necessary, but I'm okay with that. We don't have to avoid perfectionism... perfectly.

40. PERSEVERANCE

When nothing seems to help, I go and look at a stonecutter hammering away at his rock perhaps a hundred times without as much as a crack showing in it. Yet at the hundred and first blow it will split in two, and I know it was not that blow that did it – but all that had gone before.

- *Jacob Riis*

Yellow and Red Rose

I often find these lines from a Jackson Browne song going through my head: "And when the morning light comes streaming in, I'll get up and do it again. Amen."

Getting up and doing it again – persevering – is the hallmark of the hero. In the folklore of countless cultures across time and space, it is what distinguishes heroes who succeed from those who do not. For example, there is Odysseus, who spent 10 years fighting in the Trojan War and another 10 getting home, arriving on the shores of his beloved Ithaca with nothing more than the rags he was wearing, and then finding his journey far from over. Or the Buddha, who meditated beneath the Bodhi Tree until he found the root of suffering and how to liberate us from it. Or Moses, who led the Jews out of Egypt and guided them for 40 years in the desert, knowing that he would not, himself, be joining them in the Promised Land.

Movies, TV shows, books, and the heroic stories of real people today continue to extol the value of perseverance. The question, however, is *how* do we persevere?

The answer is embedded in nearly every Hero's Journey story. Though heroes may begin their journeys alone, they pick up advisors and companions along the way without whom they could not complete their missions.

This lesson came home to me following the theft of the award I won by attorneys who had represented me in a medical malpractice trial. After months of misdirection, I learned that their excuses for why I hadn't received my award were all fabrications. I made a dramatic attempt at coercing them to pay me, but it failed.

I needed help. I remember telling my girlfriend, "I need a smart guy who hates lawyers. I need the Angel of Death."

The next morning, I went out for breakfast, where I spotted my commuting buddy, Ted, at a corner table. Ted, a bitterly humorous man, was a retired attorney. Following his own legal debacle, he had quit the profession. On the commuter train, we'd often exchanged tales of woe and fantasized about retribution. We briefly collaborated on a screenplay for a comedy/horror film we planned to call *Kill All the Doctors and the Lawyers*. If the Angel of Death was not available, I figured, Ted was the next best thing.

He gestured for me to join him, and I caught him up on what had happened. He swept his cup and plate aside, brushed away some crumbs, then spread a paper napkin out in front of him. Fishing a pen from his shirt pocket, he drew a small box at the top of the napkin. In it he wrote my name. "You're the general." He winked. "Or the commander-in-chief, if you prefer."

Then he drew a sequence of boxes and lines on the napkin, mapping out a command structure and plan of attack for getting my money back. "You break the problem down into components and you give each guy a piece of it. Then you go after *all* the components. You don't know which strategy is going to work, but it doesn't matter as long as some of them do. And you control the flow of information." He smiled. "Plus, I can be in the background, show you how to snipe at 'em."

After breakfast, we headed back toward my apartment. On the way, we ran into a neighbor and I told her my story. "You know," she said, "I've got a friend who might be able to help. He knows *everybody*. I'll give you his number and let him know you'll be calling."

"That would be terrific," I said.

And so the campaign began. I followed The Napkin for two years. It took several attorneys and detectives, a Manhattan D.A., a grand jury, and many others to bring my former lawyers to justice, but eventually they were both disbarred and sentenced to long prison terms. Perseverance paid off and justice was done.

When we are traversing difficult times, we all need advisors and companions in order to persevere. As Ted guided me, I now guide clients, helping them break their problems into manageable pieces, strategize plans of action, and assemble the teams they need to accomplish their goals. Some find advisors and companions in support groups for difficulties such as addiction, divorce, depression, grief, or medical illnesses. Others find them in their churches, temples, clubs, and similar social and spiritual organizations. Sometimes, support teams are created ad hoc.

Like Ted, as my clients persevere in their journeys, I often continue on in the background, offering course corrections as needed. But my most important role is simply to encourage them, regardless of the challenges they face, to get up and do it again.

Amen.

41. POSSIBILITY

The only way to find the limits of the possible is by
going beyond them to the impossible.

- *Arthur C. Clarke*

Orange Nasturtium

POSSIBILITY: MORE POWERFUL THAN A LOCOMOTIVE

During much of my childhood, I lived in the realm of possibility: machine intelligences, aliens, mutants, future worlds, alternate pasts. Infinite possibilities.

My first science fiction book was Isaac Asimov's *I, Robot*. I was 10 when I found a copy at a Temple Sinai rummage sale. It opened the universe to me. Soon, I was wandering over to the adult section of the library every week, taking out as many science fiction books as the librarian would permit. I also haunted the local pharmacy's rack of science fiction and mystery novels, trying to figure out how best to allocate my 50-cent allowance. By my early teens, I had amassed a collection of several hundred science fiction books and had read many more.

Around the time I discovered Asimov, I decided I wanted to be a "space scientist," a dream that carried me all the way through my first year of engineering school. By then, I had stopped reading science fiction – I'd put away childish things – but my love affair with it never really ended. Twenty years later, I was in a PhD program in English, and to take a break from the dry, abstract, literary theory that English Studies had devolved into, I revisited the stories I had read as a boy. It was like starting a new romance with an old lover.

I was one among many boys and girls whose interest in science was catalyzed by science fiction. The list of inventions and discoveries that came into being because science fiction writers imagined them – and children who read their stories or watched them on television became engineers who built them – is long. *Star Trek* alone inspired cell phones, video conferencing, speech recognition, tablet computers, medical imaging, hyposprays, memory cards, biometrics, wireless earpieces, 3-D printers, machine translators, flat-screen televisions, and directed-energy weapons. Other contributions of science fiction include space flight, scanning for habitable planets and alien life, biodomes, computers, robots, artificial intelligence, virtual reality, and the multitude of products derived from these technologies.

At least as important as its technological influences is science fiction's re-imagining of human potential. In the introduction to her gender-bending novel *The Left Hand of Darkness*, Ursula Le Guin describes how science fiction can expand our ideas of human possibility. "If you like you can read it, and a lot of other science fiction, as a thought-experiment. Let's say (says Mary Shelley) that a young doctor creates a human being in his laboratory; let's say (says Philip K. Dick) that the Allies lost the second world war; let's say this or that is such and so, and see what happens…. Thought and intuition can move freely within bounds set only by the terms of the experiment, which may be very large indeed." Rod Serling's '60s series *The Twilight Zone* is one example among many whose thought experiments explored sociopolitical realities and possibilities that conventional media suppressed. To bypass the censors, Serling migrated scripts about bigotry, gender roles, government oppression, politics, and war to distant planets, future times, or alternate versions of the present.

Although it has its share of "escape" fiction, the science fiction genre also contains some of the most thought-provoking works in all of literature. On a scale more ambitious than most conventional fiction, science fiction not only asks but also posits answers to the largest questions: How did this universe come into being? How will it end? Where does consciousness come from? What is its purpose? How will *we* end? Who will replace us?

Science fiction inspires us to reach not only for the stars, but also deeply within. In this way, it overlaps with psychotherapy, another way for us to boldly go where we have not gone before.

In today's insurance-managed world, psychotherapy has been categorized as just another medical modality. But as science fiction is more than space operas, robots, time travel, and aliens, psychotherapy is more than "behavioral health." Psychotherapy, too, is about making the "impossible" not only possible, but probable, through acts of imagination. The psychotherapy treatment room is a laboratory for a different kind of thought experiment. Clients ask: What if I were to test *this* limit, take steps down *that* path, plunge into *these* waters? Over time, they become emboldened to do what their parents, teachers, or peers had convinced them was impossible.

Christopher Reeve, the actor who played the omnipotent Superman, once said, "So many of our dreams at first seem impossible, then they seem improbable, and then, when we summon the will, they soon become inevitable." You don't have to be Superman, a therapist, or even a science fiction fan to actualize your possibilities. All you need is an act of imagination and the will to sustain it.

42. PURPOSE

He who has a why to live for can bear almost any how.
- *Friedrich Nietzsche*

Pink and Orange Rose

PURPOSE: ARCS

More than things, more than work, more, even, than love, a sense of purpose can guide us through fortune's sometimes outrageous slings and arrows and steady the turbulence in our lives.

The necessity of purpose underlies almost every drama ever created. A recent, and poignant, example of this is Martin Scorcese's movie *Hugo*, in which each character ultimately finds his or her purpose, sometimes in unexpected ways. "I'd imagine the whole world was one big machine," young Hugo Cabret says to his new friend Isabelle. "Machines never come with any extra parts, you know. They always come with the exact amount they need. So I figured if the entire world was one big machine, I couldn't be an extra part. I had to be here for some reason. And that means you have to be here for some reason, too."

Having a purpose motivates us to put one foot in front of the other and to make the sometimes heroic effort to overcome internal and external forces that threaten to drag us down. Purpose has led many of my clients out of terrifying struggles: A heroin addict and former sports hero whose life was dominated by wanting to "make a mark on the world" discovered his affinity for working with mentally retarded adults. An alcoholic became a drug abuse counselor, paying forward what she had learned in recovery. A severely depressed client was freed from a cycle of repeated suicide attempts by discovering her desire to help abused women. Many others with similar arcs to their stories, the arc of the Hero's Journey, propel their lives through purpose.

Sometimes purpose seems inborn. My youngest brother, Paul, found his sense of purpose when he was 5. My mother had left him at a petting zoo at the local mall and when she came back, all the animals were gathered around him as if he were St. Francis of Assisi. From then on, he knew he wanted to be an "animal doctor." Today, he's a world-class veterinary surgeon.

My own sense of purpose has shifted several times. When I was 7, my purpose was to help the United States beat the Russians in the newly declared "space race," an impetus that carried me to Cornell University's engineering school.

By the time I finished my first year in engineering, however, purpose had started to shift. Radicalized by the War in Vietnam and opened up by the Woodstock-era counterculture, I discovered gifts for creative work. I finished college an English major.

After graduation, I followed my girlfriend to New York City. Running out of money, overwhelmed by the breadth of job choices in the Classified section of the *New York Times*, I stayed up one night writing about my talents, experience, and aspirations, hoping for an epiphany. Toward dawn, I had one: Writing, itself, was something I could do for the rest of my life without ever exhausting its possibilities. During the next few years I developed a blend of memoir and journalism I called "slow journalism," hoping, as a virtual outcast myself, to give voice to the real outcasts of the city I had landed in and thereby fashion my own identity.

This writerly sense of purpose held strong for nearly 20 years, carrying me first to artist colonies, then to the creative writing program at Boston University, and eventually to a PhD program in English at the University at Albany. There, purpose shifted again following a near-death experience, which brought me to what I do today as a therapist and artist.

Now, with the number of years in front of me far fewer than those behind, I sense an inward turning, an integration of all my apparently separate purposes into one, and a drive to become, before I die, what is the birthright of us all: a fully realized part of the everything that is Hugo Cabret's "big machine."

For me, purpose has mainly been linked to career, but purpose can be found in many other places, such as families, communities, spiritual pursuits, creative activities, volunteering. Purpose can even be as simple as deciding to act with kindness and generosity every day.

Purpose can be revealed suddenly and lucidly, or it can evolve and refine itself over time. Like every living thing, human beings lean toward self-actualization, and the sense of purpose we outwardly display at any stage may be no more indicative of its final incarnation than a caterpillar's form presages the butterfly it will become. What's important is to identify our purpose's inner core, embrace it, and then to enact it in whatever way we can.

43. RESILIENCE

The art of living lies less in eliminating our troubles
than in growing with them.

   - *Bernard M. Baruch*

Orange Dahlia

Along with perseverance and a sense of purpose, to successfully traverse the Hero's Journey that describes our lives we also need resilience.

Resilience is the ability to bounce back. In a physical object, it is elasticity. In an ecosystem, it is the system's capacity to rebuild itself. In a person, it is recovering from adversity. Without resilience we are overcome by obstacles and tend to give up in the face of hardship. With it, although we still feel the pain of defeat, we don't let it keep us down.

Resilience in materials is intrinsic, but in people it is a dynamic quality. Like a muscle, it can be damaged by too much stress or can atrophy if neglected. But it also gets stronger with exercise. In my therapy practice, I see many people whose resilience has been beaten down or in whom it was never developed. After we deal with the problems that brought them into therapy, much of our work together is about creating a more resilient approach to life.

Over time, I've been developing a program for building resilience. It focuses on skills that help us adapt to change. They fit into four categories: (1) creating a resilience-friendly environment, (2) finding support from systems and individuals, (3) enhancing problem-solving ability, and (4) increasing emotional adaptability.

Environment. A first step toward creating a safe, resilience-friendly environment involves cat hairs. The term "cat hair" comes from an experiment with lab rats designed to determine whether rats are genetically programmed to fear cats. Researchers placed young rats who had never been exposed to cats in a cage and then monitored their playfulness. Initially, the rats played together freely. Then the researchers took the smallest cat stimulus they could think of, a single cat hair, and dropped it into the cage. Soon, the rats stopped playing and ran to the edges of the cage, trembling with fear. After a few hours, the researchers removed the cat hair and continued to monitor their subjects, but even days later, the rats showed signs of fear. And they never returned to their baseline playfulness.

Fear can leave an indelible imprint on us, too. If it's not addressed consciously, we also respond to our "cat hairs" with fight/flight/freeze responses. "Cat hairs" can rule our responses to jobs, relationships, conflict, authority figures, and many other aspects of our lives, inhibiting self-actualization. Fortunately, unlike rats, we can learn to distinguish when a cat hair is a sign of real danger and when it's just a hair. Then we can protect ourselves from actual threats and soothe our fearful responses to triggers.

Support. Another component of resilience-building is establishing and maintaining close relationships. Trauma, addiction, low self-esteem, depression, and anxiety all feed on isolation. We are social animals, and separation from the pack weakens our ability not only to thrive, but sometimes even to survive. Friendships, family, support groups, spiritual groups, and group activities that validate our interests and identities can steady us when we're under stress and act as safety nets when we stumble.

Problem solving. Perhaps the most powerful factor in building resilience is looking for the silver lining in the cloud. Questions like "What can I learn from this?" and "How can going through this make me a better person?" provide leverage on our problems and prevent them from consuming us.

Emotional adaptability. Adversity can disconnect us from our creative and spiritual selves. Tapping into calming practices such as meditation, prayer, yoga, and tai chi help center us when we have been dislodged. Creative activities bring important latent parts to life. Awakening our spiritual and creative sides helps us move on from adversity with a fuller response to whatever lies ahead. The ability to empathize with others and to give with an open heart also enhances emotional adaptability. In the moments when we feel most depleted, giving to others lets us become our best selves. This principle underlies healing practices in many indigenous cultures, where the shaman chooses a sickly boy to become his apprentice. The boy becomes strong through healing his people, but he must continue to heal others in order to stay healthy himself.

Over the course of a lifetime, my own resilience has come from incorporating all these modalities. I have found strength in therapy and close friendships, connection in community and family, self-discovery in my artwork and writing. Participating in a Buddhist sangha has become gratifying in ways I'd previously associated only with intimate relationships and close friendships. And stepping into my best self each morning as I walk into my therapy office allows me to continue being the wounded healer who remains healthy by helping others to heal, and who stays resilient only as long as he assists others in developing their own resilience.

44. RISK

And the day came when the risk to remain tight in a bud
became more painful than the risk it took to blossom.

- *Anaïs Nin*

Asiatic Lily

RISK: REWARDS

When they first arrive at my office, most of the people I see are in a state of comfortable discomfort. Although we come to psychotherapy wanting change, most of us change only when the risks of changing are lower than the risks of staying the same.

This is not hard to understand. Our patterns, defenses, and coping mechanisms are well-practiced and our anxieties so familiar that we often confuse them with who we really are. It's as if we are saying that without our neuroses, we wouldn't be ourselves. Our self-actualized versions can seem, at times, like a dream. And yet we are more than our neuroses, much more, and something compels us to risk becoming that dream.

In therapy, risks almost always generate rewards. More often than most of us are willing to acknowledge, the same is also true outside the therapist's office – and sometimes crucially so.

The method I most often use to encourage risk is "the experiment." Together, my clients and I identify actions they can take between our current session and the next that have the potential to move them a step closer to where they want their lives to go. Experiments are typically actions they feel some anxiety about taking, but when they do, regardless of the outcome, they feel a sense of progress. These experiments are, by definition, always a risk, but we make an effort to ensure that the risk is manageable – not so small that doing the experiment won't matter, but not so large that it is too scary to attempt.

I came to "the experiment" through Gestalt Therapy training and first used it with a young artist at Massachusetts College of Art during my counseling internship there. His life was fraught with addiction, depression, dysfunctional relationships, and hostility from his family. He had come to MassArt with high hopes, but the strain of the life he was living put him on a direct path to flunking out. He needed more help than counseling alone could provide, but he had learned, in most areas, not to ask for it. So we devised an experiment: He agreed, on one day in the upcoming week, to ask for help in a situation where normally he would refrain.

A couple of days later, he stopped at a McDonald's for a hamburger and coffee. Looking around, he noticed that all the tables were occupied. It was a windy, bitterly cold day. He shrugged, buttoned up, and was about to eat his burger while he walked to work, but then he remembered the experiment. Instead of leaving, he asked another young man, sitting alone at a table for four, if he could join him. The young man said "yes," and my client and he ended up having a lively, animated conversation.

This small experiment was a turning point. My client realized not only that he could ask for help, but also that he was as entitled to it as anyone else, and that when he asked, he was more likely to get it than he had supposed. Over the course of the school year, with help from several sources, he was able to quit using drugs, leave a job where his coworkers expected him to be the "party boy," go back to working as an artist, and resolve major issues with his family. Even his lover quit drinking and drugging.

Since then, I have witnessed many clients take small, experimental risks that empowered them to tackle the much larger ones they faced. They have taken the risk of leaving relationships, of getting married, of quitting a job, of going back to school, of moving out of their parents' houses, of stopping the addictive behaviors on which they have depended, and of facing fears and trauma they've spent a lifetime avoiding. In each case, the risk of staying the same eventually exceeded that of embarking on the unknown.

My own life, too, has been a series of long shots, many of which have not "paid off" in a conventional sense, but which have shifted me in ways I needed to shift. Leaving the safety of engineering school led to years adrift, but also to my becoming a writer and photographer. Quitting technical writing to return to grad school indirectly resulted in a near-fatal event in an Albany hospital, but that episode also nudged me toward becoming a psychotherapist, a career that has paid off in ways I am still discovering. There have been many other risks and many other rewards.

I have come to trust risk. Not all risks are wise, but even the foolish ones can put us in motion when we're stuck in comfortable discomfort. And when we jump into the water and have to swim, we eventually find our way to somewhere new.

45. Self Love

You, yourself, as much as anybody in the entire universe,
deserve your love and affection.

- *Unknown*

Pink Dahlia

Self Love: Evolution

In my more troubled youth, I was often told that to truly love anyone, I needed first to love myself. This advice, though well-intentioned, set up an unhelpful dynamic. Loving myself seemed as much like actual love as masturbation was to sexual intercourse – a solitary substitute for the real thing. Why would I want that?

In my mid 20s, while riding the subway from Manhattan to Brooklyn, I had an insight: To love ourselves, we need first to experience *being* loved – not loved with strings attached, not intermittently loved, and not loved blindly, either, but loved for who we actually are, like Dr. Seuss loves: "You are you. Now, isn't that pleasant?" Or Mr. Rogers: "You've made this day a special day by just your being you. There's no person in the whole world like you. And I like you just the way you are." Without this loved-at-the-core experience, loving ourselves is difficult to manage.

About 10 years ago, I received a variation of the "love yourself" advice, but this time I was better equipped for it. I had just completed five days at a Buddhist retreat. While there, I had been liberally sprinkled with what the retreat leader, Thich Nhat Hanh, called "dharma rain," and some of it had soaked in. As we were leaving, a newfound friend said to me, "David, next time you think you need something from someone, try giving it to yourself first." My initial response was still to see "giving it to myself" as emotional masturbation, but I knew her to be a wise woman; what she was telling me, I realized, had to mean something else.

My receptivity to her advice was enhanced by finding a different kind of love in the temporary community Thich Nhat Hanh and his monks and nuns had helped us create. There, I'd felt warmth and affection from nearly everyone I had met, shared meals and meditations, spoken heart-to-heart with one of the monks on a hillside overlooking the dining hall. Feeling loved had become broader and more available than it had ever seemed before.

I understood, finally, that receiving unconditional love from one person was not the only way to water the seeds of self love. I felt, viscerally, that I was not alone; on the contrary, I was fully embedded in the universe. The sun, the clouds, the trees, many human beings, as well as most of the creatures of the earth, in some way expressed their love, and I was among their recipients.

As the weeks passed, I tried to heed my newfound friend's advice. Although at first nothing much happened, after a while I noticed a tiny droplet of warmth each time I tried to give myself something I thought I needed from someone else. Then one day, in the midst of grieving the suicide of a close friend, the love from the "lover" part of me toward the part that was hurting changed from a trickle to a flood. I was overcome by a love unlike any I'd previously experienced, an instant transfusion of compassion and caring pouring from a deep, wise-seeming part of me into a part that had always felt bereft.

Later that year, my lover and beloved parts united. Driving home after a 14-hour day of internship work and counseling psychology classes, I reflected on a particularly moving session I'd had that afternoon with a young artist whose mother had just died. And it struck me that I, who was so long separated from self love, was becoming someone who could love unconditionally and help my clients learn to love themselves.

In the years since then, it has become increasingly easier to love myself. A key to self love has been consciously encouraging awareness and openness toward both the parts that can offer love and the parts that need loving. I can feel loneliness and then truly comfort the lonely boy who still lives inside me, as if I am developing, within me, an ever-present father figure who can help "Davey" feel understood, cared for, and accompanied. As I learn to love myself more fully, I also become further empowered to love, care for, and accompany others.

Although the first rush of self love can be dramatic in its intensity, the preparation is often gradual. At first, it may appear that nothing is happening. But just as water can hover at its boiling point for a long time while energy is still being applied, eventually a quantum change occurs. As the water is transformed into steam, the unloved places inside us can transform into something whole and beloved.

46. SILENCE

Everything in life is speaking in spite of its apparent
silence.

- *Hazrat Inayat Khan*

Blue Pansy

SILENCE: OUTSIDE IN

About silence I am tempted to say, "I have nothing to say." And yet I do.

I have always had an ambivalent relationship with silence. As a boy, silence was someplace I retreated into to get away from the literal and emotional noise of my family. I spent most of my non-school time isolated, either holed up in the basement, performing experiments, or on my top bunk, reading science fiction and comic books. I fantasized about the silence of space, wishing I could shut my ears as easily as I could my eyes.

Toward the end of high school, radicalized by the Vietnam War, I tried to break out of silence through writing about my newfound outrage. In college, an impulse to engage more interactively with the world got me hitchhiking across the U.S. and Canada. In my early 20s, I moved to New York City, where I became a reporter, photographer, and teacher, forcing me to speak to strangers. In my late 20s, a priest I knew observed that I came alive in relationships. Yes, that's right, I thought. How could I have failed to notice?

Still, I also craved silence, which was in short supply in Manhattan. I relished my time in the darkroom and at my L.C. Smith typewriter, grinding out newspaper articles, street people stories, and a book about American folk music.

It was a noisy world and I was noisy inside. I moved to Brooklyn to get away from the screech of the elevated subway, yowling cats, blaring sirens. But dogs barked, sirens still blared, garbage trucks growled. I retreated again.

I spent a year traveling and living in artist colonies, then moved to Boston for a graduate program in writing. I first lived in Cambridge, which seemed manageable compared to New York, but there, too, the din was too much. I drifted slowly up the coast, progressively distancing myself from urban centers. For a couple of years I lived at the end of a dead-end street by a river in Medford, but barking dogs pushed me on to the Salem Willows, stone quiet when I'd arrived in the fall, but a bedlam in the summer, when the nearby '50s-style amusement park opened for business again.

I returned to grad school and took an apartment in a rural area east of Albany, still seeking solace in what I hoped would be relative silence. But noise pursued me even there. When hunting season was in full swing, I felt like I was in a war zone.

My relationship with noise took a different turn after my near-death experience, which remains the most still, silent place I have been, a place of true emptiness, stripped even of the static of a conventional self. Since then, I've been more focused on turning down my internal noise, which is almost always louder than the noise of the outside world.

Silences like those of the basement lab, the darkroom, and the writing desk are still important to me, but more essential is entering, when I can, an inner silence. This, it turns out, is the silence I have always craved. Meditation, with its continual centering/distraction/centering cycle, has been helpful, and so has adopting a friendly curiosity about my response to noise, both inside and out: Why does that noise, that thought, that memory, that emotion draw my attention? What is it stirring? The more important noise, I've come to see, is mine to control.

An example: Recently, someone whose old car had a bad muffler moved into my neighborhood. He frequently parked beneath my bedroom window. At 6:20 a.m., he started the car, and I woke immediately. For 10 minutes, he idled the engine, occasionally racing it, then sped off. For the first three days I lay in bed fuming for two hours, helplessly trying to figure out how to *get that noise to stop*, at last groggily rising from my bed, consumed by resentment, at 8:30 a.m. On the fourth day, I realized that my new neighbor and his noisy car were keeping me up for the first 10 minutes, but it was my own anger that kept me awake for the next two hours. After that, sometimes I woke up and sometimes I slept through the muffler noise, but I no longer saw it as an oppressive intrusion. It was part of the environment, a piece of impermanence, and it, too, would pass.

Silence has become a kind of haven again, but not an isolating one. From my refuge of internal silence, I can also better hear what others are saying without words, without even gestures, but with their hearts, and pay fuller attention to the still, silent places in them, where acceptance incubates and from which positive change emerges.

47. STILLNESS

In the midst of movement and chaos, keep stillness
inside of you.

  - *Deepak Chopra*

Water Lily

STILLNESS: BELLS AND WATCHES

At a retreat I attended years ago, I was introduced to the concept of the Mindfulness Bell. At random times throughout each day, someone sounded a bell, and we all had to stop what we were doing and take three slow, abdominal breaths. We halted in mid-sentence, mid-stride, mid-chew, as if we were in a big game of freeze tag. At first this practice annoyed me. I was in the midst of spiritual evolution, damn it. Stop interrupting! But before the retreat ended, I embraced these "interruptions."

In my first counseling internship a few months later, I worked with a young woman whose list of mental health and life problems was long and troubling. She heavily abused alcohol, moved from one destructive relationship to another, was grieving her parents' ugly divorce and her own traumatized childhood, and was finally seeing her father's drinking for what it was, alcoholism. Because she had no financial support, she also worked long hours at a restaurant where drinking and drugging on the job was the norm. She was angry, depressed, anxious, and lonely.

In therapy, she brought up as many as 10 problems in a session. She spoke derisively of her four previous therapists and rejected nearly every therapeutic intervention I tried. I realized I was on the road to becoming idiot therapist number five if I didn't think of something different. At the start of our next session, unsure what else to do, I handed her my watch and asked her to be still for one full minute. Only after the second hand completed its appointed rounds could she begin.

What ensued was unlike our earlier sessions. She spoke more slowly and she tended more often to stick with one topic. Consequently, she also dug deeper. We were, we both realized, finally doing therapy! After that, we began each session with my handing her my watch. A few weeks later, she brought her own watch. A few weeks after that, she didn't need it.

To emulate the "watch effect" in her outside life, I taught her the three-breath meditation I'd learned at the retreat, instructing her to treat any bell, beep, or other sharp sound she heard as if it were the Mindfulness Bell.

Over the next few months, we worked through many of her issues. By year's end, she'd quit her waitress job, stopped using drugs and alcohol, was setting better boundaries with both parents, and had found other adults to mentor her. In our parting session, I asked her what, of all we had done together, had been helpful. I was expecting, I suppose, to be thanked for my brilliant insights and clever use of the Gestalt and Solution-Focused therapeutic techniques I had been trying out, and I'd prepared myself to deliver a falsely modest, "Oh, I just helped a little. You did the work." So I was surprised when she replied, "That thing with the watch. And the breathing thing. They really helped me."

Learning to be still in the midst of the chaos of her life, even briefly, had permitted her to reevaluate her choices. Each time she paused for three slow breaths, she had a chance to feel her feelings, check in with her intuition, and rethink what she was about to do. At a street corner on the way to work, hearing the Mindfulness Bell of a car horn, she could think, "I don't really want to waste my time partying tonight." About to leave for a bar, pausing on the first ring of her cell phone, she could see how the evening would play out and decide, "Not this time." Hearing a siren blare in the midst of pangs of guilt or shame, she could choose to forgive herself.

Today, I still suggest practices to clients that create stillness, even if only for a minute, so they, too, can interrupt their habitual thoughts, feelings, and actions and discover they have other options. I also continue to use these practices myself. When I step into my office, I stop for a moment and imagine putting on an invisible jacket worn only by my best self. Brief meditations throughout the day help me shift gears between clients, return to center when I'm knocked around emotionally, and reinhabit that best self again.

In some ways, the small stillnesses that happen throughout the day, *in media res*, seem more powerful than daily sitting meditation. They are meditations with eyes open, fully in the world, and each can provide a touchstone wherever we are, whatever we are doing.

48. SUFFERING

The deeper that sorrow carves into your being, the more
joy you can contain.

  - *Kahlil Gibran*

Sunflower 'Moulin Rouge'

SUFFERING: SO IT GOES

Helen Keller once observed that the world is full of suffering, but also of the overcoming of it. Yet it is also full of suffering that is unrelieved.

In my profession, I see, and empathetically experience, a wide variety of misfortunes and maladies. In a given week, I might witness any of the following: anxiety, depression, abuse, neglect, illness, financial collapse, addiction, poverty, loss, grief, relationship struggles, shame, jealousy, rage, loneliness, disappointment, despair, hopelessness, past and present trauma, and, potentially, suicide. Sometimes I am able to help people overcome this suffering. Sometimes, all I can do is accompany it.

This is obvious. But what may not be as apparent is that my helplessness to relieve much of what I witness is a source of my own suffering. As an antidote, I remember a quote by Gandhi that a former supervisor posted on his door: "Whatever you do will be insignificant, but it is very important that you do it."

I think of suffering I have endured, and how the difference between bearable and unbearable has almost always been the presence of someone who was willing to ride along with me no matter where my suffering took us. I think, too, of great humanitarians such as Mother Theresa, who would pass through crowds of thousands whose suffering she could not hope to alleviate, but whose bearing witness to it still made a difference.

The idea of *accompanying* is still central to my approach. But, still, I want to do more, when and if I can. So I have also tried to clarify the kinds of suffering I might actually be able to allay.

Only occasionally can I help with suffering caused by physical and circumstantial difficulties. Sometimes I can persuade someone to get medical attention. Sometimes I can help someone figure a way out of difficult circumstances. But these kinds of direct interventions are relatively rare in my field. It is with self-inflicted suffering, the suffering we add to the pain of our injuries and losses, that I have more sway.

I have witnessed astonishing triumphs over physical and circumstantial suffering. As a species, we seem fairly well-equipped to bear pain, poverty, adversity, illness, injury, and losses. Paradoxically, many of us find less palpable suffering – the suffering created within our hearts and minds – the most difficult to endure. Luckily, this kind of suffering is not only more prevalent but also more amenable to actual relief.

As a therapist, I can help people to cope with things they cannot change and to accept limitations and losses. I can teach them new skills for managing emotional states, for responding in a more fulfilling way in relationships, and for actualizing potentials that have lain dormant within them. I can also help them find allies, separate from detractors, and break out of dysfunctional patterns that heretofore were imprisoning. When they learn to do these things, they become more resilient, so that if life kicks them in the gut again, although they may still feel the pain, recovery comes more quickly and easily.

Compared to the magnitude of the world's suffering, what I do may seem insignificant, but in the lives of the people I am able to touch, Gandhi was right: it *is* important that I do it. At the end of most days, I feel confident I have fostered some good that might not otherwise have occurred. This is immensely satisfying and it also gives meaning to my own suffering, without which I may never have attempted this work.

I know that understanding suffering will be a lifelong endeavor, but there are a few things I've learned that will, I think, feel true until the end. The most important is that striving for a time of no suffering only creates more suffering. We often think: "If only I had this or didn't have that, then I would be happy. If only I had a girlfriend. If only I had a job. If only I didn't have this illness. If only my husband would... my children would... I could..." But suffering is inevitable. None of us is likely to be spared illness or the loss of a loved one or a difficult turn of fortune, and nobody escapes death. Attempts to avoid *all* suffering only add to our anxiety about potential loss, encourage futile efforts to keep things as they are, or create obsessive striving for "perfection" when "good enough" is often something to be grateful for.

There is nothing unfair about that. This is the nature of what Buddhists call *samsara*, the endless cycle of birth, suffering, death, and rebirth.

So it goes.

49. TRUST

Trust is the first step to love.
   - *Munshi Premchand*

Galliardia 'Arizona Sun'

TRUST: EXPERIENCED INNOCENCE

When I was in Boy Scouts, we all had to memorize the Scout Law: "A Scout is trustworthy, loyal, helpful, friendly, courteous, kind, obedient, cheerful, thrifty, brave, clean, and reverent." Even then, I noticed that "trustworthy" was first on the list.

Trust, as an admirable quality, shows up everywhere. We want to trust our lovers, our leaders, our judgment, our friends, our gut and, says the inscription on each coin of the realm, our God. When I ask clients to list the five characteristics they most want in a relationship, trust appears more frequently than anything else.

We come out of the womb trusting implicitly, but according to developmental psychologist Erik Erikson, we begin to question trust as early as our first year of life.

Violations of trust teach us to distrust. When our trust is betrayed, we feel pain, so we create guardians to protect us from more pain, and when our pain has been great, the guardians we set up are powerful and always on red alert. But because these guardians are not invariably accurate or efficient, we may continue to attract untrustworthy people into our lives, and we may also project untrustworthy qualities onto those who are deserving of our trust. Each time we re-experience distrust, our guardians grow stronger. They can lock us into a self-fulfilling prophesy of distrust that further convinces us of the need for their protection. We may reach a point where we so identify with our guardians that distrust becomes the norm and we hide our hearts from everyone.

T.S. Eliot once wrote, "What loneliness is more lonely than distrust?" When I ask people who seem isolated by their distrust how they discern who is trustworthy and who is not, they can't give me an answer. They've been burned so many times they have given up trying. Sometimes, as their therapist, the first trusting relationship they have is with me.

In good therapy, each side honors the true nature of the other, and together we construct a container that permits difficulty, and even conflict, to occur without jeopardizing the relationship. In our initial meeting, I explain to clients that therapy is a collaborative process. I stress how important it is to tell me if I've done something that angers or disappoints them. If I've done or said anything potentially harmful, a corrective response from me is essential. If the client has misperceived what I did or said, clarifying what actually happened is equally vital. I let them know I will take responsibility for my part in any conflict between us and will stay with the process until we work it through.

Nearly two centuries before Erikson's observations on trust, the Romantic poet and illustrator William Blake depicted the passage from an innocent, child-like trust into embittered distrust in his books of poems *Songs of Innocence* and *Songs of Experience*. In *Songs of Innocence*, published in 1789, we hear the joyous cries of England's innocent: "When the meadows laugh with lively green, / And the grasshopper laughs in the merry scene; / When Mary and Susan and Emily / With their sweet round mouths sing "Ha ha he!" The mood of *Songs of Experience*, published five years later, is much darker: "Cruelty has a human heart, / And Jealousy a human face; / Terror the human form divine, / And Secrecy the human dress."

In his later works, Blake portrays a synthesis of Innocence and Experience that reclaims Innocence, transcending the effects of disappointment, mistreatment, and betrayal. Blake scholars call this state "Organized Innocence." In Organized Innocence, we can feel the joy of "Ha ha he!" even in the face of the darkness inherent in the human heart, and it cannot be subverted by further Experience.

Attaining a healed, resilient state akin to Organized Innocence is one of the main goals of psychotherapy, and it can only occur in the presence of trust. Trust! Trust! Trust! is the fundamental therapeutic motto: Trust the therapist, trust the client, trust the process. Establishing this three-way trust is the first directive of psychotherapy. Without it, healing in relationship is unlikely to occur.

In this mutually trusting environment, the protective wall of distrust born of Experience can be remodeled. Instead of a monolithic defense that continually hardens against connection, it can morph into a semi-permeable membrane, allowing *in* only those who are trustworthy, filtering *out* those who are not. Over time, as we become proficient at recognizing trustworthiness, we form more durable connections with those worthy of our trust and build stronger boundaries to protect us from those who are not. We learn to Trust! Trust! Trust!: Trust ourselves, our own processes of discernment, and those we care about.

This, I think Blake would agree, is the essence of Organized Innocence.

50. Uncertainty

The quest for certainty blocks the search for meaning.
Uncertainty is the very condition to impel man to unfold
his powers.

 - *Erich Fromm*

Sea Holly

Uncertainty: Negative capability

Perhaps the greatest fear is of uncertainty.

This fear is great because it's so encompassing. We're uncertain about what will happen in our relationships, the economy, the climate; how people see us; how an undertaking will go; how our children will do in school, and in life; what will become of us as we age. And no matter who we are, how healthy we seem to be, how much we know, how wealthy we have become, or how much power we have, we are uncertain about our own end – when it will occur, what will cause it, whether we will suffer, how we will be remembered, what will happen afterward. The only thing we can *really* be certain of is uncertainty.

Some of us manage uncertainty by replacing it with certainties. Like good Boy Scouts, our motto is "Be prepared." My father, a Boy Scout leader for many years, lived by this credo. He had duplicates, and in some cases triplicates, of all the vital parts of the devices in our house. We had a sump pump to keep the basement dry, a backup sump pump in case that one failed, and a backup of the backup… just in case. Stacked beside his workbench were two or three replacement motors for the washing machine and the dryer. Shelves in a nearby closet overflowed with duplicate faucets, belts, hoses, clamps, fasteners, TV and radio tubes, and other spare parts. We could have stocked a small hardware store with all that stuff.

Others follow the proverb, "Hope for the best but expect the worst." We have a positive attitude, but we also try hard to be ready should disaster strike. We keep our spare tires inflated, save for a rainy day, buy bottled water when the forecast calls for a snow storm, back up our computers, purchase long-term care insurance.

But what about things we can't prepare for? Or the "worsts" we could never anticipate?

The Romantic poet John Keats offered an answer in what he called Negative Capability, the capacity to be "in uncertainties, mysteries, doubts, without any irritable reaching after fact and reason." Negative Capability neither assumes nor anticipates the best or the worst, but instead recognizes that most things cannot be known in advance.

Since I first ran across Mr. Keats' concept as a college sophomore, Negative Capability has helped me to "Be prepared" not by trying to anticipate all possibilities or to have multiple contingency plans, but by having faith that I can handle whatever does happen. What it comes down to is learning to like surprises.

Liking surprises became an explicit goal when I was in therapy myself. I'd recently returned to the Boston area and my girlfriend had came to visit for a long weekend. By Monday, we'd been fighting for days. We teetered on the edge of breaking up, and I was trying to persuade her to come with me to my scheduled therapy session. I called my therapist, described what had been going on, and asked if he needed to know whether she'd be joining me there. He replied, "It doesn't matter, I like surprises." Inwardly, I reminded myself how much I *didn't* like being surprised, but it also occurred to me how liberating his viewpoint must be.

That conversation came to my aid years later, shortly after I began my first counseling internship at Massachusetts College of Art. Although I had only two counseling psychology classes under my belt by the time the internship began, when I accepted it I'd assumed I would be dealing mainly with familiar college student problems such as roommate issues, homesickness, relationship issues, academic difficulties, and maybe drugs or alcohol. Instead, within a month I had encountered not only these kinds of problems, but also suicidality, psychosis, the aftermath of a murder, personality disorders, and many other serious problems. It seemed impossible to predict or prepare for what my young artist clients might bring to a session.

Then I remembered my former therapist's "I like surprises" remark. Unsure what else to do, I vowed to regularly repeat that phrase to myself until it became my new motto. To my astonishment, it helped! Over the next few weeks, I was increasingly able to remain in "uncertainties, mysteries, doubts" without pushing the panic button. From that more equanimous state, I could more confidently assure my clients that "we can sort this out," even when how to do so was far from clear.

Negative Capability continues to foster a feeling of competence in dealing with the unknowable. I still don't always welcome surprises, but when they come, I can greet them with an ever-increasing composure that accompanies my fearful self like a wise and trusted friend.

So far, so good.

51. UNIQUENESS

Never forget that if there weren't any need for you in all your uniqueness to be on this earth, you wouldn't be here in the first place.

 - *Buckminster Fuller*

Yellow Daffodil

Uniqueness: Blooming

Discovering who I uniquely am has been a long and circuitous journey. Growing up, I often felt like a misfit, the Ugly Duckling who was different from, and therefore inferior to, everyone around me. I knew I was "smart," but I was also the shy and introverted one surrounded by extroverts, the would-be intellectual surrounded by would-be athletes, the Jew among Christians. My adult life has been a gradual and uneven unfolding of talents that were mostly disregarded during childhood.

As a boy, I spent a lot of time hiding out in the world of science fiction, and the stories I was most attracted to were about mutants. In these tales, mutants were usually persecuted by those around them, though they ultimately turned out to be the crest of the next wave of human evolution. Like the mutants, I vacillated between devastatingly low self-esteem and a fragile grandiosity. I also became a kid scientist, starting my private studies first with collections of rocks, bugs, and magnets, and then later moving on to chemistry, electronics, and model rocketry. By 11, I was doing high school science on my own. By high school, I was researching personal projects in the science and engineering library of the University at Buffalo. I had "future scientist" written all over me.

By my late 20s, I was living in a house in Brooklyn near Pratt Institute, a college for artists and architects. I'd gone from kid scientist to engineering student to English major to construction worker. I was writing, taking pictures, teaching kids, and helping to renovate the house we lived in. And I felt lost.

One of my housemates was a few years older than I was and had been self-sufficient since he was 17. He had walked many walks in his 35 years – the Navy, business, construction, short-order cook, an assortment of other jobs. Now, he was an architecture student at Pratt, and he seemed to delight in what he did there. One day, as we sat together at the kitchen table, I complained about how disconnected my own career seemed. "It's all so fragmented," I lamented.

My housemate had been showing me a model of a conference center he had designed, a beautifully executed architectural sculpture. He tapped a loose wooden panel into place. "I felt the same way you did until I found architecture," he said. "Then, everything came together."

He smiled and clapped me on the shoulder. "You'll figure it out."

In his *New Yorker* article "Late Bloomers," Malcolm Gladwell contrasts artists such as Pablo Picasso, whose genius was acknowledged early in his career, with those like Cézanne, who did his best work late in life and only then received widespread recognition. "On the road to great achievement," Gladwell wrote, "the late bloomer will resemble a failure: While the late bloomer is revising and despairing and changing course and slashing canvases to ribbons after months or years, what he or she produces will look like the kind of thing produced by the artist who will never bloom at all." Early bloomers, he observed, hit the ground running, but late bloomers need support as, through trial and error, they discover how to realize their talent. "Prodigies are easy," Gladwell explains. "They advertise their genius from the get-go. Late bloomers are hard. They require forbearance and blind faith."

Late blooming occurs not only with artists, but with anyone whose nature is to discover his or her purpose through trial and error. As a therapist, I often encounter late bloomers. They are men and women who have much more potential than they've been able to actualize. Their growth has been stunted not because they lack ability, but because their latent talents were never recognized and encouraged. Without support, these late bloomers, too, may never blossom.

My housemate found architecture at 35, and decades later he's still practicing. It took me until I was 50 to find my way to psychotherapy. But like him, in this profession I have discovered that the threads of my varied careers have come together into a tapestry. I see that I'm neither an Ugly Duckling nor a mutant, and that my history is not a series of false starts. Instead, I am a late bloomer.

Although I actually know very little about botany (I had to consult a plant-identification forum in British Columbia to learn the names of the common flowers I've made into mandalas), in another sense I have found my vocation as a gardener. Because I have bloomed late, I turn out to have a talent for fostering the uniqueness of others by helping them find the right soil and conditions not only to blossom, but to thrive.

52. WILL

Where there's a will, there's a way.
 - *Unknown*

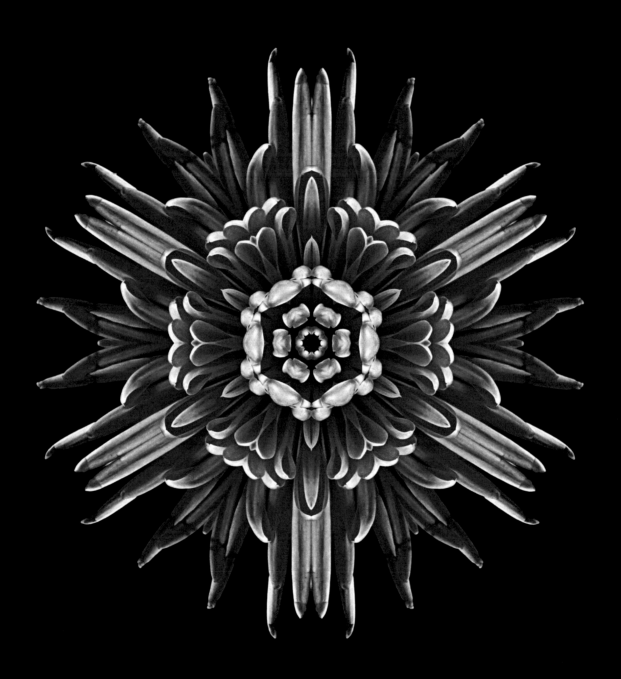

Violet Chrysanthemum

WILL: BREAK ON THROUGH

There are many ways psychotherapists can help people. We can provide validation, emotional support, and encouragement; identify dysfunctional patterns and devise strategies for overcoming them; and sometimes even inspire. But often, to fully surmount difficulties, there is also a decisive moment when *will* comes into play. Will raises the apparently defeated fighter from the mat, enables the runner to move out from behind, keeps us going when everything in us says we can't continue. Will is often the difference between triumph and failure, not only in myth and story but also in our personal struggles.

Will is the key to breaking through what psychologist Jim Grant calls the "Spell ceiling." Our collections of past injuries, and the mistaken beliefs and patterns we have created to protect ourselves from them, can be regarded as a trance-like Spell that controls much of what we think, feel, and do. Until we awaken, our Spells command us to repeat our patterns. Acting in ways that defy our Spells weakens them, and we get stronger. The Spell ceiling occurs just as the Spell is about to yield. At that point, the Spell often puffs itself up and, like the Wizard at the end of *The Wizard of Oz*, tries to scare us back into our old ways. We have killed our Wicked Witches, but the Spell wants to send us on another mission anyway, because that's all it knows how to do. By then, however, we have changed. Like the characters in the film, we have reached the threshold of our true selves without realizing it.

It's not difficult to spot the Spell ceiling if you know what to look for. In therapy, people who rarely have problems focusing suddenly space out. Those who are always on time forget their appointments. "It feels like I'm going backwards," some clients suddenly complain. Outside therapy, old patterns reemerge.

It's at this critical juncture that *will* comes into play. If we succumb to the Spell now, we lose ground and it resumes its role as puppeteer. If, instead, we muster up our will and resist returning to old patterns, the Great and Powerful Oz is revealed to be merely an old man whose only power is illusion.

When the hold of the Spell is broken, we are free to redirect the energy we have been supplying to it, fueling our own growth. But the Spell has not thrown in the towel. To continue to stay ahead of it, we need to keep doing what got us through the Spell ceiling. Coupled with ongoing awareness, will is, once again, essential.

To help myself and my clients stay above our Spell ceilings, I use a monitoring tool called the Personal Craziness Index (PCI)[1]. In each of ten major life areas, the PCI catalogs three indicators of how we act when we are Spell-free. Then we track the most significant ones every day.

If we notice we are slipping back into Spell-influenced behaviors, chances are good our Spell is setting us up for another fall. What's nice about the PCI is that corrective actions are built into it. All we have to do is resume whatever it is we've stopped doing, and we'll most likely get back on track.

For instance, suppose that in the "Health" category we wrote that when we are doing well, we go to the gym three times a week, cook our own meals, and sleep at least seven hours per night. Although each of these actions alone may seem unimportant, as indicators that we're on top of our Spells they are invaluable. When we notice we're skipping the gym, picking up junk food, or skimping on sleep, we become aware that we're also drifting toward a Spell relapse. At this stage, because we've given up only a little ground, pulling ahead of our Spell again is easy: we *will* ourselves to return to the gym, cook our meals, and get more sleep, and the downward slide reverses.

Catching our Spells before they gather enough strength to pull us under is much easier than breaking through the Spell ceiling again. In 12-step recovery programs, the phrase "fake it till you make it" expresses the idea of using will to assume new, more self-actualizing behaviors and attitudes. The PCI helps us "fake it till we make it" at a stage where the quantity of will that's needed to keep our personal craziness at bay is minimal.

As the old saying goes, where there's a will, there's a way.

Use your will. Take the way.

---

[1] See Appendix III, "Personal Craziness Index," from *A Gentle Path Through the Twelve Steps*, by Patrick J. Carnes.

APPENDICES

APPENDIX I: FORGIVENESS MEDITATION

By Jack Kornfield

To practice forgiveness meditation, let yourself sit comfortably, allowing your eyes to close and your breath to be natural and easy. Let your body and mind relax. Breathing gently into the area of your heart, let yourself feel all the barriers you have erected and the emotions that you have carried because you have not forgiven – not forgiven yourself, not forgiven others. Let yourself feel the pain of keeping your heart closed. Then, breathing softly, begin asking and extending forgiveness, reciting the following words, letting the images and feelings that come up grow deeper as you repeat them.

Forgiveness from others. *There are many ways that I have hurt and harmed others, have betrayed or abandoned them, caused them suffering, knowingly or unknowingly, out of my pain, fear, anger, and confusion.* Let yourself remember and visualize the ways you have hurt others. See and feel the pain you have caused out of your own fear and confusion. Feel your own sorrow and regret. Sense that finally you can release this burden and ask for forgiveness. Picture each memory that still burdens your heart. And then to each person in your mind repeat: *I ask for your forgiveness, I ask for your forgiveness.*

Forgiveness for yourself. *There are many ways that I have hurt and harmed myself. I have betrayed or abandoned myself many times through thought, word, or deed, knowingly or unknowingly.* Feel your own precious body and life. Let yourself see the ways you have hurt or harmed yourself. Picture them, remember them. Feel the sorrow you have carried from this and sense that you can release these burdens. Extend forgiveness for each of them, one by one. Repeat to yourself: *For the ways I have hurt myself through action or inaction, out of fear, pain, and confusion, I now extend a full and heartfelt forgiveness. I forgive myself, I forgive myself.*

Forgiveness for those who have hurt or harmed you. *There are many ways that I have been harmed by others, abused or abandoned, knowingly or unknowingly, in thought, word, or deed.* Let yourself picture and remember these many ways. Feel the sorrow you have carried from this past and sense that you can release this burden of pain by extending forgiveness when your heart is ready. Now say to yourself: *I now remember the many ways others have hurt or harmed me, wounded me, out of fear, pain, confusion, and anger. I have carried this pain in my heart too long. To the extent that I am ready, I offer them forgiveness. To those who have caused me harm, I offer my forgiveness, I forgive you.*

Let yourself gently repeat these three directions for forgiveness until you feel a release in your heart. For some great pains you may not feel a release but only the burden and the anguish or anger you have held. Touch this softly. Be forgiving of yourself for not being ready to let go and move on. Forgiveness cannot be forced; it cannot be artificial. Simply continue the practice and let the words and images work gradually in their own way. In time you can make the forgiveness meditation a regular part of your life, letting go of the past and opening your heart to each new moment with a wise, loving kindness.

APPENDIX II: NEW TIMES AND SHAGGY DOGS

In 1975, I lived in a fifth-floor walk-up on Manhattan's Upper West Side. The apartment was noisy, oppressively hot, and roach-infested. I was working hard at becoming a journalist but had found little paid work. I diligently read the magazines I hoped would publish me, among them *The Village Voice*, *The New Yorker*, *Esquire*, and *The Atlantic*. But they were well-established, and I knew my chances were slight. So when I discovered *New Times* magazine, I got excited. Their left-leaning, investigative approach appealed to me, and they seemed to be open to up-and-coming freelancers. Hope renewed, I sent in a subscription check for $15.

A week later, I got an offer from *New Times*. If I sent in the enclosed postcard, I'd get a free copy and be entered in a lottery for a Hawaiian vacation. I could also subscribe at the reduced rate of $10. From the vantage point of my fifth-floor walk-up, Hawaii sounded good, so I mailed in the card, but I left the box for subscribing blank, since I had already paid full price for my subscription. A week after that, I got another vacation postcard from *New Times*. There was nothing saying I couldn't enter the lottery twice, so I sent that one in, too, once again leaving the "subscribe" box unchecked.

My first issue came, and memories of Hawaiian vacations began to fade as I wracked my brains for a story I could submit to them. A week later, I got another copy of the same issue. I didn't give it much thought – just the free issue from the postcard offer, I figured. A week after that, I got the second issue from my actual subscription and yet another copy of the first one. The second postcard's freebie, I assumed.

But the following week, I received a subscription bill and another duplicate issue, followed a week later by another subscription bill and yet another duplicate. I left the redundant copies of the magazine by the mailboxes and sent the bills back in their prepaid envelopes, along with a polite note informing *New Times* that I was already a paid subscriber and only wanted one copy of the magazine.

Every two weeks my regular issue of *New Times* faithfully appeared, as well as a copy of the previous issue and a subscription invoice, followed a week after that by another duplicate magazine and another duplicate bill. With increasing irritation, I returned each invoice to the subscription department, along with an explanatory note.

After a couple of months, their letters started to get nasty. One week *New Times* admonished me for taking advantage of their generosity. A week after that, they sent me a duplicate admonishment. A week later, they vaguely impugned my honesty. A week after that, identical vague impugning. You get the idea. For a while, I continued to dutifully return each letter and invoice, by then retaining a carbon copy of my accompanying note to use for the duplicate bills I knew I'd receive in the following weeks. As my irritation grew, however, I eventually just let the invoices pile up.

More months went by. Then one day I got a letter in a pink, red-edged envelope with a different return address. Inside, the author sternly reprimanded me, threatened my credit, and warned that if I didn't pay immediately, he would turn the case ($10) over to a collection agency. A week later, I got an identical pink, red-edged envelope and another threatening letter.

No more Mr. Nice Guy! I packed up all the accumulated letters, all the envelopes, and all the subscription postcards I could find and wrapped them in a piece of blank paper. On it I wrote, in red, felt-tipped pen, in crazed uppercase letters with lots of underlining, "STOP NAGGING ME!!!! I NEVER ASKED FOR THESE F**KING MAGAZINES!!! HERE'S YOUR INVOICES. YOU KNOW WHERE YOU CAN PUT THEM!!!!!!!!!" I thought that might get their attention.

A week later, my regular issue of *New Times* arrived, along with a duplicate copy of the previous one, and a week after that, another duplicate. I tossed the duplicates in the trash.

A week after that, I got a postcard from *New Times*. They acknowledged their error, apologized, assured me that the problem had been rectified, and even offered to extend my subscription at a reduced rate.

Triumph!

Then a week later, I got a postcard from *New Times*. They acknowledged their error, apologized, assured me that the problem had been rectified, and even offered to extend my subscription at a reduced rate....

I told you it was a shaggy dog story!

Appendix III: Personal Craziness Index

Adapted from *A Gentle Path Through the Twelve Steps,* **by Patrick Carnes**

Listed below are 10 suggested categories for the Personal Craziness Index. If some of these categories don't fit your situation, you can substitute others that do. To create your own Personal Craziness Index:

1. Under each category, write three indicators that you are in a good place – list either things you *do* that keep you in positive territory, or things you *don't do* that also show you are doing well. For example, under Health/Hygiene you might list "exercise 3x per week" as something you do to stay fit, or "don't eat junk food" as a reminder to avoid doing something unhealthy.
2. Now choose seven indicators to track. These should be the ones that best demonstrate you're maintaining your defenses against personal craziness. At the end of each day, give yourself a score, where "0" is "I'm not doing any of the positive things / am doing all of the negative things" and "7" is "I'm doing all the positive things / not doing any of the negative things." Track your scores daily. **NOTE**: You get a "0" for days you don't bother to check!
3. If the numbers start dropping, reverse the trend by doing the positives and avoiding the negatives. When your Personal Craziness Index is restored, your personal craziness will, likewise, diminish.

Health/Hygiene	Recreation
1.	1.
2.	2.
3.	3
Housing	**Family**
1.	1.
2.	2.
3.	3.
Transportation	**Friends**
1.	1.
2.	2.
3.	3.
Work/Money	**Group activities**
1.	1.
2.	2.
3.	3.
Hobbies/Interests	**Spirituality**
1.	1.
2.	2.
3.	3.